# THE CORPORATE TRANSLATOR

# The CORPORATE TRANSLATOR

## A GUIDE TO *Nonsense Words* IN THE OFFICE

MIKE MANCUSI

Andrews McMeel
PUBLISHING®

The authorised representative in the EEA is Simon and Schuster Netherlands BV, Herculesplein 96 3584 AA Utrecht, Netherlands. (info@simonandschuster.nl)

Andrews McMeel Publishing
a division of Andrews McMeel Universal
1130 Walnut Street, Kansas City, Missouri 64106

www.andrewsmcmeel.com

26 27 28 29 30 VEP 10 9 8 7 6 5 4 3 2 1

ISBN: 979-8-8816-1025-8

Library of Congress Control Number: 2026935654

Editor: Kate Zimmermann
Art Director: Holly Swayne
Production Editor: Kayla Overbey
Production Manager: Julie Skalla

FSC www.fsc.org
MIX
Paper | Supporting responsible forestry
FSC® C005010

For my parents, Vinny and Marian—
who taught me what actually matters in life and
gave me the sense of humor to survive the rest

# Contents


Introduction 1

A Brief History 2

The Copycat Culture 3

Avoiding Uncomfortable Truths 5

A Culture of Confusion 7

Meet the Corporate Translator 8

How to Use This Book 11

PART 1

CORPORATE TRANSLATIONS 13

Strategy, Execution, and Vision 14

Performance and Execution 20

Meetings and Communication 24

Leadership and HR Jargon 29

Process and Operational Excellence 36

Tech, Innovation, Growth!!! 🚀🚀🚀🚀 39

Corporate Drama and Chaos 42

Soul-Crushing Metaphors 45

Acronym Hell 50

Nonsensical Job Titles 56

## PART 2

## SITUATIONAL TRAINING 59

Interviewing for a Job 60
Starting a New Job 77
Performance Reviews 83
Raise and Promotional Conversations (Rejections) 87
Team Meetings 91
Company Announcements 97
HR and People Operations 109

## PART 3

## CORPORATE TRANSLATOR TIPS 117

Operational Navigation Protocols
(Navigational Tips to Protect from the Facade) 118
Strategic Mindset Enablement Framework
(Adopt the Translator Mindset) 127
Action Items to Drive Adoption
(How to Improve Workplace Communication) 131

Conclusion 133

# Introduction

Most people reach a point in their corporate lives when they hear words like *synergy* and *bandwidth* and pause for a moment, thinking, *Wait, what is everyone talking about?* or *Does anyone actually know what they're saying?* or maybe even *Why are we talking to each other like we're in* Star Trek*?*

If this is you, or it has been, then come with me on this journey. By the end of this book, the Corporate Translator will have answered all the existential questions that plague your nine-to-five.

While this realization can feel unsettling, it's also an important one. Once you've reached the point where you feel like you're taking crazy pills, or maybe suspect that the CEO slipped some Corporate Kool-Aid into your morning coffee, you're finally ready for the truth: *It's all made up.* It's a ruse. An elaborate game. Kind of like *The Hunger Games,* but with everyone's careers on the line.

The way people talk in corporate culture is a direct reflection of that. Words aren't meant to explain what's happening; they're meant to sound impressive, make the business seem more valuable than it is, and leave everyone in a vast amount of disarray and confusion. Corporate language—or, as I call it, "Corporate Speak"—is built to create an illusion to help everyone dance around uncomfortable truths. That's corporate life in a nutshell.

## A BRIEF HISTORY

In order for us to identify the origins of Corporate Speak, we need to rewind back—way back—to the Ice Age, when Neanderthals roamed the Earth. The first-ever recorded Corporate Speak phrase was used when two local cavemen went out hunting for fish. One caveman went out armed with a spear, the other with a net. After hours and hours of fishing, the two men came up empty-handed. Both of these men had newborn babies at home and were beginning to feel the pressure of needing to provide.

The sun was going down, and the two men were exhausted. The reality of another hungry night was weighing heavily on them. Then, just when all hope was lost, one of the cavemen had a brilliant idea. A light bulb went off in his head, and he knew how to solve all their problems. He turned to his partner and said five words that altered the trajectory of human history:

"Should we try leveraging AI?"

The two men celebrated the idea. They went on to catch twenty-six thousand fish in forty-five minutes by harnessing the power of AI. They triumphantly returned home and founded the company Rivercorp.ai—*streamline your streams*.

. . . Anyway, I made all that up, but it sounded *a little bit* believable there for a second, didn't it? That's the power of ***Corporate Speak:*** in this case, combining terms with just a little bit of mystery, like *leverage* (page 17), with historical gravitas to give them the kind of impact that might catch the attention (and money) of others. If that sounds a little cynical, then let me put it this way: Your employer may be using language like that to attract investors and push you to agree to take on more job responsibilities without a raise. But Corporate Speak goes both ways. You don't have to just absorb their stories; you can craft your own mythical history, describe your own responsibilities and job title in a way that captures their interest in situations where they might normally get defensive, and ultimately "level the playing field" (to use a popular strategy incorporating needless sports analogies . . . see page 26) by speaking to your employer in their own language. All you need to do is start understanding it.

First, let's look at the origins of Corporate Speak, which I, in all my years of training, have managed to boil down to three main pillars:

Pillar #1: A copycat culture
Pillar #2: A desire to avoid uncomfortable truths
Pillar #3: A culture of confusion

Let's delve into each to develop a more nuanced understanding of how this practice evolved, and why.

**The Copycat Culture**

Pillar #1: Put simply, most companies don't want to develop the recipe for their own sauce (***translation:*** It's hard to come up with ideas). They just want to understand how the competitor or a similar company—ideally on the other side of the pond—grew to be successful and then copy that model.

Coming up with your own ideas and creating your own unique culture is a lot of work, which sounds exhausting. Work? Who the hell wants to do that? That's why so many companies feel exactly the same, no matter what it is they actually "do."

Think about when you walk into a McDonald's, a Wendy's, or a Burger King. Ostensibly they all offer different kinds of food and different experiences, but functionally they are slight variations of the same thing: fast food recipes focusing on hamburgers. Beyond packaging, their menus are almost interchangeable (burgers, fries, shakes), with similar prices and near-identical vibes.

It takes a lot of work, innovative risk, and entrepreneurial spirit to really want to break the mold. It's much easier to be handed a playbook, then tweak it just a little to say that it's a big new idea. Founders will see a post on LinkedIn from a CEO with the title "5 Tips That Helped My Business Scale from $1M to $500M in ARR" and then make that their bible. It's a lot easier to do that than to put in the work to understand the unique problems the business faces and how to solve them.

This is not limited to CEOs. This winds up happening in every department. Sales leaders learn from other sales leaders, marketers from other marketers, HR people from other HR people, and so on. They learn their best practices, tools, templates, models, and even their unique varieties of Corporate Speak from their peers.

People hear their manager, mentor, or some social media personality they like speak this way, and they think, *Wow, that sounds really smart; I will sound equally as smart if I speak that way, too!* This is how Corporate Speak winds up spreading like a virus.

Businesses are operating the same way. Following the same playbook. And sure, it can be soul-crushing. But predictability means this kind of language is easily interpreted across industries. Can you imagine a corporate Tower of Babel, with every fast-food hamburger restaurant developing its own kind of jargon? That would really limit transferable skills across industries! And it would be at least mildly inconvenient for you, too.

## Avoiding Uncomfortable Truths

Pillar #2: Businesses are afraid to be honest. They need to keep a large group of people motivated for long periods of time. Sometimes motivation really doesn't make sense, given the situation. Therefore, Corporate Speak becomes necessary.

Generally, you can keep people bought in by making them feel like:

A) They are valued.
B) The company will be successful.

The reality is usually closer to:

A) They are a source of value extraction.
B) The company has massive holes.

Have you ever tried to motivate someone by saying:

> "Our goal is to get as much output from you as possible while paying you as little as we can—oh, and we might lay you off at any time."

That's probably not going to move the needle (page 18) for most people, now is it?

It's much easier to say something like:

> "We care deeply about our stakeholders and invest heavily in their growth and development."

Or consider this golden nugget. Have you ever tried to rally the troops by saying:

> "Our product is mediocre, and we're nowhere near profitability, so the odds of long-term success diminish by the day."

That's not exactly a great recipe for Corporate Kool-Aid (page 47).

A much better one sounds like:

> "Our revolutionary product, paired with our best-in-class go-to-market (GTM) strategy, will drive unlimited scale."

Much more compelling, isn't it?

It's easier to say:

> "We don't have the budget to give you a raise."

Than it is to say:

> "We know we can get away with underpaying you for a lot longer."

And so, all this Corporate Speak exists to avoid uncomfortable truths and disguise the fact that people are being motivated to accept situations that don't benefit them. Because if employees truly understood the reality of their situation, they'd be more likely to realize they shouldn't be working for the company's benefit—rather they should be working for *their* benefit. And that's more than mildly inconvenient for a company that wants to scale up!

### A Culture of Confusion

Finally, Pillar #3: Mass confusion is often used as a leadership tactic. Employers at the top of the food chain generally want people to know exactly what they *want* them to know. They're most likely to say things like: "The company is doing great." "Your job is secure." "Everything is just swell." They want everyone living in that curated reality—surface-level positivity only, please—while ignoring the red flags hovering over everyone's day-to-day like a sleep paralysis demon.

You can hide all that negativity behind obligatory buzzwords that don't make any practical sense. Just say, "We're smashing our targets," and let people blissfully go about their day without asking too many questions. Ideally, everyone leaves the team meeting thinking, *I'm not totally sure what just happened, but it* sounded *good!*

Questions bad! Buzzwords good!

Even better—the preferred outcome for most employers—is when people collectively shrug it off. They go into a team meeting where their manager says:

***Corporate Speak:*** "We had a very strong quarter, but we really need to get our ducks in a row and drive efficiency to stay on track for our yearly targets."

***Translation:*** "We did okay this quarter, but we're still massively behind."

A large portion of employees walk out saying, "I'm not sure what that really means, but I'm not getting paid enough to care."

In this case, confusion leads to disinterest. And when people aren't interested in the real answers, the "Everything is great!!!" narrative becomes incredibly easy to maintain. No poking, no prodding—just shrug it off and get back to work.

## MEET THE CORPORATE TRANSLATOR

Sounding a little bleak so far? I suggest you push your worries aside. Enter me: the Corporate Translator. I exist to translate this kind of nonsense into plain English. My official legal distinction is an "office service animal," which means I have the ability to enter any professional environment to promote the flow of open communication. And much like other service animals, while I'm working, you can't touch me—not even the CEO. I also do provide a kind of emotional support. However, within the pages of this book and without truly putting aside my professional obligations, I'll let you in on a secret, which is that my bottom line isn't bandwidth (page 20), deliverables (page 23), or even ROI (page 52): My ultimate goal is helping people in an office talk to each other like actual human beings. And while that means I'm generally applauded by employees and silently hated by managers, the fact is I'm able to accomplish that simply by being a voice with no skin in the game, here to help people understand what's really happening and how to navigate it.

This book is for anyone at any stage of their corporate career. Maybe you're ten years in and wondering why your manager sounds like a Klingon. Maybe you're fresh out of college and trying to decode your first all-hands meeting. Or maybe you're a senior manager who just wants to improve your relationship with direct reports.

Communication is the foundation of any healthy relationship. Honesty and open dialogue build trust, empathy, and real connection. Sadly, these principles are often lost somewhere between "alignment" and "cross-functional functioning." It's time to bring them back, along with our humanity. That is what I, the Translator, am here to do.

If my previous metaphors haven't worked for you, you could try envisioning me as a human app that sits in your meetings as an overlay (this works especially well for programmers). Picture yourself at a conference table, hearing your boss fire off some Corporate Speak, and then turning to Siri and saying, "Hey, Siri, what the hell did he just say?" Then I'd happily share her much clearer, more concise explanation that breaks everything down into plain English.

Over time, corporate meetings have devolved into a maze of jargon that no one actually understands. That's where I come in—to help normal humans strip the nonsense from the buzzwords and finally understand what's really happening in the workplace. Come along with me on a crash course in garbled, bizarre, euphemism-filled non-language and get ready to break it down into actual words that might come out of a human mouth. And we'll do it with humor, because comedy is the only remedy for the soul-suck that is corporate culture. My goal is to bring humanity back into the workplace, and laughter is the conduit that makes that possible.

## *The Translator in Action*

Here's a real-life example of how the Translator operates within the corporate landscape. I was pulled into a one-on-one where an employee, Bob, was meeting with his department head, Tim, to discuss "taking on additional responsibilities." Bob was the most tenured representative on the team and had been asking for a promotion for six months. Here's how it went:

**TIM:** So, I wanted you to be the first to know that your manager, Anne, has resigned. It was a totally amicable situation, and we're parting under good terms.

**BOB:** *looks to Translator*

**TRANSLATOR:** Anne got another job, and the rest of the management team was caught incredibly off guard by it. Now they're freaking out.

**TIM:** Um, no—this was a highly mutual transition, and we're incredibly appreciative of the value Anne added throughout her tenure—

**TRANSLATOR:** Yeah, they're panicking.

**TIM:** . . . Anyway, while these transitionary periods can be difficult, it also creates a compelling opportunity for you to accelerate your impact within—

**BOB:** Great, so you're promoting me?

**TIM:** Well, yes. We're going to promote you to team lead while we evaluate our options.

**TRANSLATOR:** They're not promoting you.

**TIM:** Yes, we are! We are happy to offer you the team lead role and give you an opportunity to showcase that you're the right person for the role.

**TRANSLATOR:** They're definitely not promoting you.

**BOB:** Great. Well, I assume I will get a raise, and how long will it take me to get the manager title?

**TIM:** We see this as a great opportunity for you to show why you are the right person for the role, so–

**TRANSLATOR:** They are expecting you to take on more work without additional pay and just hope that it eventually works out.

**BOB:** You know what? I think I'm all set. You can hire externally.

The Translator bows. End Scene.

This is a job well done, by the way: The employee understands exactly what they're signing up for, and no one has used language for a nefarious purpose. If Bob wanted to sign up for more work and the possibility of an eventual title change, who am I to stop him? But now he has the tools to make an informed choice himself.

## HOW TO USE THIS BOOK

This book has three sections:

1. **Corporate Translations:** What do these words mean? How are they used in sentences? What do those sentences mean? What is happening?
2. **Situational Training:** Corporate interactions are full of buzzwords and spin. The Translator will help you understand what's happening and how to respond.
3. **Corporate Translator Tips:** You'll see how you can improve your workplace communication and put an end to the nonsensical crisis.

# PART 1

# CORPORATE TRANSLATIONS

Read on for a list of the most common Corporate Speak words and practical definitions for each. They will be organized into subcategories related to the context in which they are typically used.

# STRATEGY, EXECUTION, AND VISION

Where is the company going? Who knows?! But here are some words that'll make you think it's somewhere good.

## SYNERGY

Originally used in seventh-grade biology to describe how two cells work together, now hijacked by corporate America to describe how two departments pretend to like each other.

***Example:***

"Marketing and Sales have had a lot of synergy recently, driving the top-of-funnel pipeline."

***Translation:***

"Marketing and Sales have been doing a good job of working together to bullsh*t their numbers."

## STRATEGY

Historically, this word was very commonly used in wartime to describe a plan of attack. Now it's more commonly used in the everyday battle that is corporate life. This is one of the most overused words in all of corporate. It's used so broadly that it's lost all meaning.

***Example:***

"What's our strategy for this?"

"I think we should restrategize our existing strategy."

***Translation:***

"Can someone please give me the illusion that we know what we're doing?"

## STRATEGIC INITIATIVE

A term used to elevate routine, everyday tasks into something that sounds visionary. If you need employees to care about something boring, just call it a "strategic initiative," and suddenly it sounds like you are piloting a mission to Mars. In reality, it refers to basic and simple stuff.

***Example:***

"The company has just begun a strategic initiative to generate pipeline."

***Translation:***

"We just pumped a bunch of money into ads because we need leads."

## EFFICIENCY

This is Corporate Speak for "DO THIS FASTER NOW."

***Example:***

"We really need to drive efficiency against our strategy."

***Translation:***

"WE NEED A FASTER STRATEGY."

## NORTH STAR

This phrase was often used by sailors who used the North Star as their guiding light. Now, it refers to a goal, whether company-wide or individual, that is so far from attainable, it literally exists in space.

***Example:***

"Our North Star goal for this year is to quadruple our revenue."

***Translation:***

"We know this will never happen, but let's just make a goal that will stress people out all year."

## OPTIMIZE

This is Corporate Speak for "MAKE THIS BETTER NOW."

***Example:***

"We really need to optimize our strategy."

***Translation:***

"WE NEED A BETTER STRATEGY."

## DISRUPTER

Being a "disrupter" refers to a business that completely reinvents an industry. The catch is that the product actually has to work—a standard many so-called disruptive companies fail to meet. More often than not, companies label themselves disrupters as a superficial way to differentiate from the thousands of other products that do the exact same thing.

***Example:***

"We need to be a disrupter in the space."

***Translation:***

"We need the space to think we are somehow better than the ten thousand other products that do the exact same thing."

## UTILIZE

This is essentially the pretentious form of the word *use*. Often *utilized* when people want to sound smart instead of just saying the normal word, which is *use*.

***Example:***

"We should utilize AI to drive automation."

"Have we thought about utilizing AI for this?"

***Translation:***

"Have we thought about using AI for this? Also, I'm very smart."

## LEVERAGE

This is an even more pretentious form of *use*. Technically it does have an appropriate application as a noun during negotiations, but it's generally used for no purpose.

***Example:***

"How can we leverage AI for this?"

"Is there a way for us to utilize leverageable AI?"

***Translation:***

"I think I'm Steve Jobs."

## AGILE

A term once reserved for professional athletes who can run a 4.5-second forty-yard dash is now somehow applied to a bunch of middle-aged people who sit at desks all day. Typically, it is used to gaslight people into thinking it's normal for the business to change directions every day.

***Example:***

> "We need to be more agile as an organization."

***Translation:***

> "We don't know what we're doing, and you need to get used to that."

## MOVE THE NEEDLE

Make progress. It literally just means *to make progress.*

***Example:***

> "How can we move the needle on this?"

***Translation:***

> "How can we make progress on this while I also use an unnecessary metaphor?"

## ALIGN

This word has been used, ad nauseam, to describe two things that need to work together.

*Example:*

> "Mark, can you please align with Chrissy on that strategic initiative?"

*Translation:*

> "Mark, can you and Chrissy go pretend to be on the same page?"

## THINK OUTSIDE THE BOX

This is generally used to acknowledge that everyone's current ideas are bad and you need to think of better ones.

*Example:*

> "In order to hit our goals, we really need to think outside the box."

*Translation:*

> "All your ideas are bad, and you should feel bad."

# PERFORMANCE AND EXECUTION

Are you doing your job well? Doesn't matter!
Here are some words that will confuse you!

## BANDWIDTH

Originally used to describe the amount of data that can be transmitted or stored on a network, this now refers to how much information or "stuff" a person can cram into their brain. It's often used to talk about someone's time or mental capacity and is almost always only mentioned when they have none for you.

***Example:***

"I'm sorry, I can't help you. My bandwidth is fully allocated."

***Translation:***

"I'm sorry, I can't help you. I'm busy and tired, and even if I weren't either of those things, I still probably wouldn't want to."

## LOW-HANGING FRUIT

Low-hanging fruit implies that there is fruit that is attainable without having to climb the tree. This phrase is often used to give the illusion that work should be easy, even in situations where it definitely won't be.

***Example:***

"After all, there is a lot of low-hanging fruit out there."

***Translation:***

"You guys should do better because work is easy."

## QUICK WINS

The natural sequel to *low-hanging fruit*. If the fruit is easy to grab, then the results should come just as easily . . . right?

***Example:***

"We need to go after the low-hanging fruit in order to get some quick wins."

***Translation:***

"We haven't really thought this through, but surely it will drive results!!"

## BEST FOOT FORWARD

This is a (faux) nice way of telling people that they need to do better.

***Example:***

"We really need to put our best foot forward on this."

***Translation:***

"Please, for the love of God, do better."

## ACTION ITEMS

The sequel to *deliverables*. Same concept but now with urgency and an inevitable, unnecessary follow-up meeting.

***Example:***

"Is everyone clear on their action items?"

***Translation:***

"Does everyone know what they're going to forget about until the next meeting when we ask again?"

## DATA-DRIVEN

This term is often used when people want to use a cherry-picked data element to support whatever narrative they are trying to push.

***Example:***

"All our goals are data-driven."

***Translation:***

"We used manipulated data to set unattainable targets."

## PIVOT

This is a (faux) nice way of telling people that they should do something different.

***Example:***

"You should pivot away from your current strategy."

***Translation:***

"Your current strategy is bad, and you should do something different."

## DELIVERABLES

This is an overly complex term used to describe the stuff you need to do.

***Example:***

"Here are your deliverables."

***Translation:***

"Here's the stuff you need to do."

# MEETINGS AND COMMUNICATION

What better way to communicate than to make our meetings sound like we're speaking a foreign language?

## PIGGYBACK

This term is used when people are going to take credit for someone else's thought. It is also by far the most visually hilarious metaphor in all of corporate. I don't get it. Are the pigs sitting on each other's backs? Is that biologically possible? Is it just one piggy's back? So many questions, so few answers.

***Example:***

"Just piggybacking on Brenda's thought . . ."

***Translation:***

"Brenda had such a good thought that I want to take it."

## PUTTING LIPSTICK ON A PIG

Just piggybacking on the piggyback metaphor, this is the second most visually hilarious pig-related analogy in all of corporate jargon. It's used to describe making something appear impressive when it's actually not.

*Example:*

"The new user interface upgrade is just putting lipstick on a pig."

*Translation:*

"Our product is bad, but hopefully a new interface will hide that."

## CIRCLE BACK

A "polite" way to tell someone you are in the process of annoying them about a certain thing.

*Example:*

"Hey, just wanted to circle back with you on this."

*Translation:*

"Hey, I'm going to keep bringing this up to you until you hate me."

## NUDGE YOUR INBOX

This is the digital version of "circling back." It means that you are going to annoy them about something, just digitally this time.

*Example:*

"Just nudging your inbox on this."

*Translation:*

"I'm going to blow up your inbox until you either quit or answer me. The choice is yours."

## TOUCH BASE

This phrase is everyone's least favorite sports analogy and a close sibling to *nudging* and *circling back*. In baseball, *touching base* means you're safe because you've physically reached the base. In Corporate Speak, the "base" represents your free time and, often, your personal space.

***Example:***

"Can we quickly touch base?"

"When can we touch base?"

***Translation:***

"Can I infringe on your time and space with an unnecessary meeting?"

## TAKE THIS OFFLINE

This phrase treats humans like malfunctioning robots. It's used in meetings when two people start discussing something they'd rather not address in public or, ideally, ever again.

***Example:***

"I don't want to derail this meeting—let's take this offline."

***Translation:***

"We should talk about this afterward, or hopefully never again."

## PING ME

Generally, this is used as a brush-off. No one takes a *ping* seriously. People ask to be pinged about things that they want to ignore until the end of time.

*Example:*

"Ping me if you don't hear from me by Friday."

*Translation:*

"Please, for the love of God, don't ever bring this up again."

## DEEP DIVE

This term is used to give the illusion that anyone will dig into a certain topic past surface-level assumptions.

*Example:*

"Let's take a deep dive into these numbers."

*Translation:*

"Let's look at these numbers for fifteen more minutes than we normally do and draw the exact same conclusion that we would have anyway."

## DOUBLE-CLICK

An absurdly unnecessary way of asking someone to go into more detail. Borrowed from computer terminology, this phrase implies that a deeper level of insight is about to be unlocked—when, in reality, nothing new is about to happen.

*Example:*

"Interesting. . . . Pipeline is down this month. Let's double-click on that for a minute."

*Translation:*

"Let's all pretend we're about to analyze this deeply when, in reality, we will talk in circles for forty-five minutes."

## LOOP ME IN

Normally, this is used when someone is eager to railroad themselves into a particular situation.

***Example:***

"Hey, can you loop me in on that email thread?"

***Translation:***

"Hey, can I hijack that email thread?"

## A LOT TO UNPACK

This phrase is typically used when someone just rambled on for way too long, and now we need to figure out what the hell they're talking about.

***Example:***

"Wow, there's a lot to unpack there."

***Translation:***

"Wow, you really went nuts for a second, and now we need to digest that."

# LEADERSHIP AND HR JARGON

Do your direct reports want open, direct, and clear communication? Sorry! The best we can do is use words and phrases that have no practical real-life use.

## LEVEL SET

This is often used to let people know that their expectations are far too high—or just wrong.

***Example:***

"I'd like to level set expectations with you."

***Translation:***

"I'd like to tell you that your expectations are insane."

## EMPOWERMENT

If management ever tells you this, you will likely have absolutely no support whatsoever.

***Example:***

"We empower our employees to be their own boss."

***Translation:***

"Go figure it out."

## CULTURE FIT

This is a very HR way to ask if someone is a weirdo.

***Example:***

"Did that candidate seem like a good culture fit?"

***Translation:***

"Do you think this person would fit in here, or are they weird?"

## ROCK STAR

A person or team who did their jobs very well for a noticeable period of time.

***Example:***

"Shout-out to our absolute rock star sales rep who hit quota this month."

***Translation:***

"This person did a good thing once."

## OPEN-DOOR POLICY

This is used to feign availability from upper management.

***Example:***

"If any of you need me, you know where to find me. I have an open-door policy."

***Translation:***

"My door is always open, so you can come in, and I can tell you that I'm busy."

## STAKEHOLDER

A broad term used to make anyone in the company feel like they have a stake in its success without actually giving them stock in it.

*Example:*

"Our stakeholders are key to our success."

*Translation:*

"You are all integral to the company's success, even though you have no equity."

## DO MORE WITH LESS

Frequently used after workforce reductions, *doing more with less* typically means the company plans to squeeze as much as possible out of the remaining employees. Having fewer employees doesn't mean there are fewer jobs—it just means fewer people are responsible for the same number of jobs.

*Example:*

"Since we are a much leaner team, we need to do more with less."

*Translation:*

"Since we got rid of a bunch of your colleagues, you now all have four more jobs each."

## CROSS-FUNCTIONAL ALIGNMENT

This is used to describe two or more departments that need to work in better synchrony. Now, why do they refer to people as *functions*? That's anyone's guess.

***Example:***

"We're working on improving our cross-functional alignment between marketing and sales."

***Translation:***

"We're going to give marketing and sales a reason to point fingers at each other."

## UNLIMITED PTO

This is a common tactic used to secretly discourage employees from actually taking time off (and to avoid paying them for unused days). A psychological effect is at play: When given a set amount, people use it; when given an "unlimited" amount, they keep postponing until they're not busy—which is never.

***Example:***

"We have a very generous unlimited PTO policy."

***Translation:***

"You'll work 51 out of 52 weeks per year and not even realize it."

## CIRCLE OF TRUST

This phrase is often used to encourage employees to put their guard down so they will divulge information that will later be used against them.

*Example:*

"Don't worry; you can be open with me. We're in the circle of trust."

*Translation:*

"Please share the gossip so I can spread it further and then tell everyone that you were the one who told me."

## PEOPLE FIRST

This is a phrase used to give people the illusion that people matter more than profit, which is true precisely zero percent of the time.

*Example:*

"We're a people-first culture here."

*Translation:*

"We care about our people's well-being until our shareholders say otherwise, and then we will sacrifice them without batting an eyelash."

## TAKE OWNERSHIP

This phrase is for when they need you to do something and not complain about it.

*Example:*

"We're really going to need you to take ownership of this."

*Translation:*

"We need you to fix this problem, and also don't be whiny about it."

## WIN-WIN

Often used to convince someone to do something under the pretext that both parties will benefit when, in fact, one of them won't.

***Example:***

"It's a win-win situation."

***Translation:***

"One of us is going to lose."

## COACHABILITY

A word typically used to judge the level of conformity a person has.

***Example:***

"Is this person coachable?"

***Translation:***

"Will this person do what we ask without being annoying about it?"

## MISSION CRITICAL

They use this to make a certain task or objective sound more important than it is.

***Example:***

"Your delivery on this is absolutely mission critical."

***Translation:***

"This is now the most important thing in the world until something else becomes 'mission critical' in a few hours."

## TRANSPARENCY

This word is often weaponized against employees to make it seem like management is being open and honest when, in actuality, it's just a ruse.

***Example:***

"In the spirit of transparency . . ."

***Translation:***

"Here's a word that will make you feel like we aren't hiding things while we hide things."

# PROCESS AND OPERATIONAL EXCELLENCE

There's no better way to strive for greatness and thorough execution than to give directions that no one understands.

## STREAMLINE

This is one of the most overused words in all of corporate. *Streamline* generally refers to a process, system, or sometimes an entire department of people that is currently incredibly inefficient.

***Example:***

"We really need our processes to be streamlined."

***Translation:***

"Our processes currently suck."

## PEEL THE ONION

This is a corporate, ELI5 ("Explain It like I'm Five") way of noting that you shouldn't make surface-level assumptions and should actually get to the root of an issue.

*Example:*

"Let's peel the onion on this and understand why people are unhappy."

*Translation:*

"Let's get to the root of this problem so that we can still do nothing about it."

## SCALE SCALABILITY

Generally used to make a certain product, offering, or company sound like it is about to grow way faster than it actually is.

*Example:*

"We allow organizations to scale."

"We're scaling rapidly."

*Translation:*

"We are giving the false illusion of rapid growth."

## SEAMLESS

Generally used to make things sound much easier than they actually are.

*Example:*

"We offer a seamless integration."

"The onboarding process is seamless."

*Translation:*

"These things will be way more difficult than we are making them sound."

## HOLISTIC APPROACH

This is used when companies try to sound thoughtful in their process when, realistically, everything is a cluster.

*Example:*

"We take a holistic approach to this."

*Translation:*

"We are just going to do a bunch of stuff and hope it works well."

## WORKFLOW OPTIMIZATION

This term is used to be intentionally vague when describing the value proposition of a product or organization.

*Example:*

"Our product provides maximized workflow optimization."

*Translation:*

"I'm having a hard time explaining what our product does, so I'll just say this vague, arbitrary value proposition."

# TECH, INNOVATION, GROWTH!!!

🚀🚀🚀🚀

The best way to tell your company's story is by using words that make it sound better than it is!

## DIGITAL TRANSFORMATION

An unnecessary way of explaining what technology is.

***Example:***

"Our solution provides digital transformation."

***Translation:***

"Our product is a technology."

## INTUITIVE

Used to make a product or service sound easier to use than it is. It implies that you should just use your "intuition" to figure it out instead of any actual instruction.

***Example:***

"We have a very intuitive interface."

***Translation:***

"This is easy to use, so please don't ask us any questions."

## FRICTIONLESS

Used to make something sound like it won't start a fire in your organization (it likely will).

*Example:*

"We offer frictionless integration into your existing infrastructure."

*Translation:*

"Our product will have your entire staff metaphorically trying to rub two sticks together in order to create a fire."

## SLEEK

Used to make Honda Accord–like products sound like Aston Martins.

*Example:*

"Our sleek user experience will maximize adoption."

*Translation:*

"Our product is incredibly basic, so you should be fine."

## GAME-CHANGING

A way to make a product sound way more impactful than it is.

*Example:*

"Our offering is an absolute game changer for B2B marketers!"

*Translation:*

"Our product should generally make life marginally better for a very specific user set."

## BEST-IN-CLASS REVOLUTIONARY INDUSTRY-LEADING INNOVATIVE CUTTING-EDGE

I'm going to do a group definition on these words because they all mean the same thing. They are arbitrary buzzwords used to make a technology sound cooler than it is. You will hear these words ad nauseam at your company's various pep rallies.

***Example:***

"Our best-in-class, industry-leading, innovative, REVOLUTIONARY technology."

***Translation:***

"Our technology is not that cool, so we're going to use these words to make it *sound* cool."

# CORPORATE DRAMA AND CHAOS

Should we, as a company, take accountability for the mess that we create? LOL, nah—but we can use intentionally misleading metaphors!

## RIGHTSIZING

Companies use this to justify layoffs as a good thing when, realistically, they just overhired.

***Example:***

"We're rightsizing the organization."

***Translation:***

"Our product is not as popular as we thought it was going to be, and now we need to adjust the workforce accordingly."

## RESTRUCTURING

Companies use this as a way to justify layoffs when, realistically, they are admitting the company is a mess and they need to tear it down to build it back up.

***Example:***

"The organization was in need of restructuring."

***Translation:***

"We put the wrong people in the wrong places, and now we just need to get rid of everyone and start over."

## REORG

This is a company admitting that the current organizational setup is not working and they need to RE the ORG before it goes under.

***Example:***

"We're having to reorg a few things."

***Translation:***

"We realized that a recognizable portion of people are bad at their jobs."

## TEMPORARY PAUSE

This phrase is the first warning sign of trouble. It's like when a tsunami is approaching and the tide suddenly pulls back.

***Example:***

"We're putting hiring on a temporary pause."

***Translation:***

"We're going to stop hiring people because we will soon, inevitably, have to fire people."

## WE'RE LIKE A FAMILY

Companies are all the worst parts of having a family and none of the good parts.

***Example:***

"We're like a family here."

***Translation:***

"You have to spend a large portion of your life with us, and we leave you with irreparable trauma while also having no loyalty to your overall well-being."

## SHIFTING PRIORITIES

If your leadership ever tells you they are *shifting priorities*, they're acknowledging that the direction they've been leading you down was entirely wrong.

***Example:***

"We're shifting our priorities to focus more on go-to-market execution."

***Translation:***

"Turns out everything we've said over the past six-plus months was wrong and we need to change all of it."

# SOUL-CRUSHING METAPHORS

The people who say these don't even know what they mean.

## BOIL THE OCEAN

This is one of the more scientifically absurd sayings in corporate jargon. It is often used to suggest simplifying something overly complex—ironically, through an overly complex metaphor.

***Example:***

"Let's shift our priorities. We don't need to boil the ocean on this."

***Translation:***

"This task is literally impossible and will drive us insane, so let's just pick easier stuff to work on."

## REINVENT THE WHEEL

Often this term is used to deter people from making too many changes.

***Example:***

"Well, we don't want to reinvent the wheel on this."

***Translation:***

"Our process is broken, but we don't want to fully fix it."

## RUN IT UP THE FLAGPOLE

In a literal sense, this would be an incredible athletic feat. In the metaphorical sense, it's primarily used by unathletic people—often to deflect accountability to upper management.

***Example:***

"I need to check if I can get this approved. Let me run it up the flagpole."

***Translation:***

"I'm going to deny this request but act like it was management's fault."

## BOOTS ON THE GROUND

A militaristic phrase used to describe getting people physically involved in the work—usually implying that real progress happens only when someone is doing the actual, often unglamorous, work. Often used by people who are not, themselves, putting boots on the ground.

***Example:***

"We need boots on the ground to move the needle on this."

***Translation:***

"We need a bunch of people to go do this work while I sit here and talk about it."

## DRINK THE KOOL-AID

This term refers to the Jonestown massacre, during which people were brainwashed into drinking a poisoned beverage. Now it refers to your CEO mind-melting you into believing in the business. It's always great when corporate uses analogies that compare the culture to a literal cult, right?

***Example:***

"We're all really drinking the Kool-Aid around here."

***Translation:***

"We're all well aware of and complicit in the fact that we've been brainwashed."

## BITE THE BULLET

This phrase originates from wartime surgeries, when soldiers were given a bullet to bite down on due to limited anesthetics. *Bite the bullet* essentially means "This is going to suck, so let's just get it over with." It's basically the older, tougher cousin of *YOLO*.

***Example:***

"The feature isn't ready, but we need to just bite the bullet and release it."

***Translation:***

"The pain of releasing this feature half-baked is probably less than the pain of not releasing it at all—so, YOLO."

## GET OUR DUCKS IN A ROW

If ducks don't travel in a neat, orderly line behind their mother, chaos ensues. Your boss is essentially the mother duck. If you step out of line, we all might wind up falling down a metaphorical storm drain. Essentially, this is a juvenile way of saying, "We need to get our sh*t together."

***Example:***

"We really need to get our ducks in a row on this."

***Translation:***

"GET IT TOGETHER."

## BUILD THE PLANE WHILE FLYING IT

This phrase is used to admit that a project is being executed without a clear plan, mostly based on improv, and has a high likelihood of crashing and burning.

***Example:***

"We launched a new product feature while it was still being coded; we're just going to build the plane while flying it."

***Translation:***

"We're going to put our customers into a half-baked feature and hope it works."

## SHARPEN THE PENCIL

Remember when people used pencils? Yeah, me neither. Anyway, this term is used to indicate cost cutting or budget reductions.

***Example:***

"I'm going to need you guys to sharpen the pencil."

***Translation:***

"I'm going to need you guys to charge me less money."

## RIGHT THE SHIP

Used when a project or initiative is failing, this implies that the direction of the ship is the problem, and not the actual ship itself.

***Example:***

"We're behind on revenue and really need to act with more urgency in order to right the ship."

***Translation:***

"We're behind on revenue because our product is subpar, but we're going to blame people's work ethic."

# ACRONYM HELL

MVP

Corporate absolutely LOVES a cute acronym. What better way to confuse people than to not even say actual words?

## OKRS

Objectives and Key Results: arbitrary goals and targets that people need to hit in a certain period of time.

***Example:***

"Our OKR for this quarter is to reduce churn by 10 percent and increase renewals by 15 percent."

***Translation:***

"Our OKR this quarter is to squeeze our customers and also update our résumés for when it inevitably doesn't work."

## EOD EOW EOM EOY

End of Day/Week/Month/Year: Why say three syllables when you can say three letters? That's the goal of these acronyms.

***Example:***

"I need this report by EOW."

***Translation:***

"I need this report by the end of the week. Also, I'm very lazy."

## KPI

Key Performance Indicator: Numbers chosen at random to track progress against unachievable goals.

***Example:***

"Our KPIs for this month are to increase prospecting activity metrics by 20 percent to lift the top-of-funnel pipeline."

***Translation:***

"Our KPIs for this month are to spam our prospects until they meet with us, or call the police."

## PIP

Performance Improvement Plan: This broadly translates to "Paid Interview Period." PIPs are used when you are underperforming and a company is defining certain criteria that you need to hit in order to keep your job. People have survived PIPs a lot, but generally, this is a eulogy that the organization is writing for you while you're still alive.

***Example:***

"We are invested in your success, and that is why we've developed a plan for you to thrive."

***Translation:***

"We're putting you on a PIP because we need legal documentation before we fire you."

## GTM

Go-to-Market: Organizational methodology for how you annoy every single person on planet Earth who is capable of buying your product.

***Example:***

"Our GTM strategy will be to leverage value-led market content across key distribution channels to drive product awareness."

***Translation:***

"Our GTM strategy is to pump social media ads to anyone who has a pulse instead of actually creating a product that people want."

## ROI

Return on Investment: "How much does this thing cost versus how much we want it?" In corporate, everything has an ROI: products, services, people, pets, family members, health care, basic human rights, etc.

***Example:***

"Have we done a quantitative analysis on the ROI that marketing has driven this year?"

***Translation:***

"Marketing is not driving results, so let's see if we can replace the department with AI."

## FYI

For Your Information: This is essentially the corporate term for "AHEM, EXCUSE ME." Very commonly used in a passive-aggressive manner.

***Example:***

"Hey, FYI, the numbers on your report don't align with the numbers that management has."

***Translation:***

"Hey, FYI, you're screwed."

## ICP

Ideal Customer Profile: This is the cohort of people across the globe who could feasibly buy your product. It's like the Insane Clown Posse of people who can be tricked into purchasing it.

***Example:***

"Our ICP is clearly defined as marketing leaders who work for Fortune 500 companies."

***Translation:***

"Our ICP is marketing people for enterprise organizations and also any breathing human who is willing to give us their money."

## QBR

Quarterly Business Review: "Let's get together once every three months to understand how behind on our numbers we are and which department needs to get yelled at." (Spoiler: It's all of them.)

***Example:***

"We're just out of QBR, and we are tremendously behind on our OKR."

***Translation:***

"We just got out of QBR, and it turns out we need to PIP half the company."

## ELT

Executive Leadership Team: "The team of people to whom we have given an acronym in order to put the fear of God in all of you."

***Example:***

"Our ELT team will be in the office this week, so let's have great energy!"

***Translation:***

"Our ELT team will be in the office this week, so please give them the illusion you're all happy here."

## IC

Individual Contributor: This directly translates to "replaceable human"—people on the lowest level who are also the first to be thrown under the bus.

*Example:*

"Congratulations to Doug, our top IC of the quarter. We really value your productivity."

*Translation:*

"Our top IC of the quarter was Doug, who we also unfortunately had to lay off because we had a bad quarter."

## SOP

Standard Operating Procedure: A standard set of rules, steps, or procedures thrown together in a document that no one will read.

*Example:*

"We developed a clearly defined SOP that will give you all the information you need."

*Translation:*

"Here's a document we created with a step-by-step process that absolutely no one will retain or follow."

## TBD

To Be Determined: Another way of telling people "we have no idea when this will be done."

*Example:*

"We are very close on our next round of funding, but the exact time frame is still TBD."

*Translation:*

"We are going to get our next round of funding somewhere between one month from now and never."

# NONSENSICAL JOB TITLES

Corporate Speak is not limited to interactions—it can also be used to embellish entire careers.

## CHIEF STRATEGY OFFICER

The executive responsible for shaping the company's long-term direction, setting priorities, and making sure different parts of the business are "aligned" on big-picture goals. How exactly is that different from the CEO? It's anyone's guess.

***Example:***

> "Our chief strategy officer is spearheading our long-term strategic initiatives to ensure alignment across all business units."

***Translation:***

> "We gave someone several hundred thousand dollars per year to spend their time in meetings talking about ideas we may or may not actually implement and to then take credit for work that other people did."

## CONSULTANT

Someone who is brought into the organization on a contract basis to point out a bunch of things employees are doing wrong, provide ideas on how to fix them, and then leave before those ideas get implemented.

***Example:***

"We engaged a management consultant to perform a comprehensive organizational review and deliver actionable insights."

***Translation:***

"We paid an external person the equivalent of your annual salary to analyze our business, give us the same recommendations that internal people have been giving us for years, and then leave before implementing any of them."

## VP OF STRATEGIC GROWTH

A senior executive whose role sounds ambitious and forward-thinking, while their actual deliverables are very hard to notice or define.

***Example:***

"We're excited to announce that our VP of strategic growth will be spearheading cross-functional initiatives to optimize our market positioning."

***Translation:***

"We hired someone with vague goals who will take credit for all the work you are doing."

## HEAD OF BRAND STRATEGY

The person responsible for making the company *sound* and *look* amazing—usually by creating lofty plans, slogans, and campaigns—while hoping no one actually measures whether it drives meaningful results.

***Example:***

"Our new head of brand strategy will elevate our storytelling to increase our market presence and establish us as market leaders."

***Translation:***

"We hired an exec-level person to make us a new website."

## HEAD OF PEOPLE

The person who was hired in order to give employees the illusion that people matter over numbers.

***Example:***

"We are bringing in a head of people to maximize our employee experience and cultivate a culture of excellence."

***Translation:***

"We hired someone to listen to your complaints and do nothing about them."

# PART 2

# SITUATIONAL TRAINING

Now let's delve into some common corporate tactics and how these words are used to leave you confused and professionally gaslit. You'll hear this language everywhere—from casual watercooler chats to company-wide all-hands meetings, one-on-ones, and even your monthly happy hour. There are always two conversations happening at once: what's being said, *and what people mean.* The Translator is here to help you understand what's actually happening and how to confidently and effectively navigate each situation.

# INTERVIEWING FOR A JOB

One of the most important parts of my job as a Corporate Translator is helping people navigate the interview process and see past the intentionally misleading buzzwords that fill every conversation. "Interviews" have become less like interviews and more like the Spider-Man meme—two parties pointing at each other while trying to out-lie one another. Candidates often embellish their résumés, and companies often embellish everything about themselves.

The "corporate embellishments," as we'll kindly call them, go both ways—which is exactly why the interview should, too. Companies should be interviewing candidates, and candidates should be interviewing the company. Don't accept information at face value. Ask for specific numbers, concrete examples, and the chance to speak with a current employee. Any employer that refuses should be just as big a red flag as a candidate refusing to provide a reference.

It's the same logic behind an organization asking for your historical performance metrics, "Tell me about a time" answers, and four references. Both sides are depicting their version of the story, and it's crucial to understand the *facts* of what's actually happening before making a decision—on both sides. This is exactly where I come in.

Here's an example. I was asked to join a conversation with Melissa, who was looking for a sales job. As eager as she was to give a new position her all, she wanted to make sure she wasn't jumping into a chaotic situation. This is how it went:

**INTERVIEWER:** We had a great quarter.

**MELISSA:** *looks at me*

**TRANSLATOR:** Their quarter exceeded the incredibly low expectations they all had.

**INTERVIEWER:** That's not true. We hit 115 percent of our revenue targets.

**MELISSA:** Great—and what percentage of your sales team is at quota for year?

**INTERVIEWER:** Well . . . we had a tough Q2 and have been playing catch-up all year . . .

**TRANSLATOR:** Less than 50 percent.

Do you see the power of good questions? Don't hear "Oh, you said things are great? Wow, sign me up!" Dig in, ask the right questions, be skeptical, and get to the truth.

Now, let's look at some of the most common interview scenarios you will encounter.

## SCENARIO 1

## THE HYPER-SCALE

***Corporate Speak:*** "We are currently scaling rapidly."

***Translation:*** "We are going to hire a lot of people and will probably have to fire a large portion of them soon."

This is a classic interview tactic: painting the (sometimes very imaginary) picture that you'll be part of a "unicorn." The word *unicorn* itself should be a red flag. You're literally comparing your company to a mythical creature that doesn't exist—but sure, tell me more about your billion-dollar vision. Anyway . . .

Rapid scaling *can* work. Plenty of companies have done it. But even in the best-case scenario, turbulence is guaranteed. Think of it like this:

Someone comes up to you and says, "Hey, we just invented a spaceship that can get you to the moon in an hour. Want a ride?"

Are you jumping in? Or are you asking at least a few follow-up questions?

Don't get hypnotized by the dangling carrot of "ground floor of a unicorn 🚀🚀🚀." Push for justification:

- "What makes you confident the company is truly at a stage where this level of scale is warranted?"
- "Have you tried to scale this aggressively before?"
- "Growth usually means higher revenue targets. How is the company planning to hit those?"
- "Please just tell me if this is going to crash and burn." (Translator's note: Not recommended.)

The point is to figure out whether they've seen this *unlimited scale* movie before—and if they haven't, why they're convinced *this* time will end with a triumphant montage instead of an apocalypse.

End scene.

## SCENARIO 2

# UNLIMITED GROWTH

***Corporate Speak:*** "In this role, you will have unlimited growth potential."

***Translation:*** "The job titles and responsibilities here are mostly made up."

"Unlimited growth" is an inherently absurd thing to say. There is *always* a cap on how much someone can grow in a company. Calling it "uncapped" is just selling you a vision—letting your brain latch on to the word *unlimited* and drift off into fantasies of becoming the next CEO of Amazon.

It's kind of like what they say about horror movies, that "your brain will envision things worse than anything they can put on the screen," but with the opposite effect.

Tell someone, "You can do anything; you can be anything," and they'll supply the best possible outcome on their own.

But that's not how corporate structures actually work. There should be a clear path, with a few possible directions depending on your goals, and real examples of people who have moved up. If they're intentionally vague, it means they're selling you a dream—and letting your imagination do all the heavy lifting.

## SCENARIO 3

# "WEAR MANY HATS"

***Corporate Speak:*** "We're looking for someone to come in who can wear a lot of hats."

***Translation:*** "We are trying to hire one person to do four jobs."

Have you ever pictured yourself wearing multiple hats? You'd look ridiculous. You'd also not really be able to move without one, or a few, falling off. Which is why it's a great metaphor. The business needs someone to juggle so many different things that they'll get executive paralysis. It means that they know they have several different holes to plug, and they want one person to plug them all simultaneously.

Whenever someone tells you they're looking for someone to "wear multiple hats," tell them, "It's not that cold outside—you could really just use one," and then bask in the uncomfortable lack of laughter. This is your career and your profession; they need to clearly define the role and the success criteria that come with it. If they can't define it, it means it *isn't* defined, and you'll end up doing multiple jobs while getting paid for one. If they can't clearly articulate the responsibilities and what success looks like, it's time to raise the red flag.

## SCENARIO 4

# "HIT THE GROUND RUNNING"

***Corporate Speak:*** "We're looking for someone to hit the ground running."

***Translation:*** "You'll be given no onboarding and expected to drive value within two weeks."

This is an athletic analogy being used in the most unathletic environment possible. Hitting the ground running would cause a multitude of lower-body injuries for most people over the age of thirty, which is very similar to what it will do to your career. You'll survive, but not without a strained Achilles tendon or two (also, you might *not* survive).

When you get an answer like that, you need to thoroughly vet the onboarding and training process and ask what milestones you're expected to hit in the first few months. "Hit the ground running" typically means you're expected to drive value from day one—no time for setup; just get to shareholder value. That can be fine, but if those expectations exist while you're not given adequate training, it's a recipe for failure (or burnout).

## SCENARIO 5

# "TAKE OWNERSHIP"

***Corporate Speak:*** "We need someone to really take ownership."

***Translation:*** "We know nothing, so we need someone who knows stuff."

"Ownership" should generally be a given with any job. Outwardly stating that they need someone to come in and "take ownership" means there is a massive hole and no one on staff who has any idea how to fill it. They're not going to give you a shovel; you'll need to have your own shovel. And what they *don't* mention is that normally the hole you'll be filling is the size of the Grand Canyon, and your shovel is really closer to a pail.

Here's another corny one-liner you can use if you want to guarantee you don't get the job:

"We really need someone to take ownership."

". . . of the *company*? Don't mind if I do!"

Who knows—maybe they'll love it. Corporate Speak and a corny sense of humor go together like peanut butter and jelly.

But seriously, they need to define what "ownership" actually means. Are processes broken and the company needs someone to fix them? Do processes not exist at all and the company needs someone to build them from scratch? Are you expected to babysit a team of people who have no idea what they're doing? Maybe all three? Probably all three.

It's perfectly fine for a company to want someone to take ownership in their role, but the expectations and success criteria still need to be clearly defined so you know what you're walking into.

## SCENARIO 6

# "GET YOUR HANDS DIRTY"

***Corporate Speak:*** "We're looking for someone who can come in, roll up their sleeves, and get their hands dirty."

***Translation:*** "Our current process is broken, and you'll need to fix it and probably fire people."

It's always fun when corporate tries to make white-collar jobs sound blue-collar. When they say to you, "We need someone to roll up their sleeves," they are basically just telling you their pipes are broken and that you need to fix the plumbing.

It's not a glamorous job—which is why they make it sound like you're joining a construction crew. It's important to vet what "getting your hands dirty" actually entails and, more important, *why* they need to get "dirty" in the first place. Is it because the person you're replacing wasn't right for the role? Or is there a larger organizational failure at play? Understanding this will help you gauge the level of reconstruction you're signing up for.

## SCENARIO 7

# ACCESS TO LEADERSHIP

***Corporate Speak:*** "You'll have direct access to our executive leadership team."

***Translation:*** "You'll have our executives breathing down your neck from day one."

Access to leadership is often dangled like a shiny carrot for people who aspire to be in the C-suite someday. They think, *Wow, I get to speak to leadership? The gods are smiling on me!* But in reality, access to leadership usually means being pulled into ELT meetings just to be yelled at for not having fixed the entire mess the last person left within your first three months.

This one usually applies more to management roles. If you're going to have direct access to senior leadership, are *they* the ones setting the goals? If so, how do they build those goals? What has the company's track record been for hitting targets over the past two years? Getting access to the ELT sounds like a blessing, but in reality, it means you'll have the fear of God put in you from day one—and God's targets are very often overly ambitious.

## SCENARIO 8

## "TRANSITIONARY PERIOD"

***Corporate Speak:*** "We recently went through a transitionary period."

***Translation:*** "Our company was a dumpster fire, and everyone left, so now we need to hire."

If anyone ever tells you the organization recently went through a "transitionary period," your spidey senses should start tingling immediately. The transitional period is corporate code for "total disaster."

Depending on the maturity of the company, a transitional period usually means they brought in a new leadership team to accomplish something big. It failed, everyone was miserable, the smart people left, and then those leaders were fired. Now they've brought in new leadership, need to hire new people to clean up the mess, and the cycle begins again.

Congratulations! *You* are the transition.

But surely this time will be different . . . right?

Don't accept "transitionary period" as an explanation. Transitions usually only happen when things are bad. No one initiates a transition because everything is great all the time. For example: How about you? Why are *you* looking for a job? Are you "transitioning" because everything was so damn perfect at your last company that you suddenly thought, *Wow, things are going incredibly well . . . You know what? I should definitely leave . . .* ?

No. Transitions come from turbulence. Make sure you understand what caused that turbulence and what has changed so that you don't have to transition again in six months.

## SCENARIO 9

## "WORK HARD, PLAY HARD"

***Corporate Speak:*** "We have a real work hard, play hard culture around here."

***Translation:*** "We're going to work you so hard that we'll need to sponsor happy hours in order to help you cope."

It shouldn't even need to be stated that a company "works hard." What employer is going to say, "Honestly, we really just take it easy around here"? None. Working hard is a given.

When they feel the need to package company culture with the phrase "We work hard and play hard," what an employer is really saying is that people work so insanely hard that they have to party just to feel alive.

Always ask about turnover rates and average tenure. Go on their LinkedIn account and see how long people stay. Work hard, play hard cultures almost always have incredibly high turnover rates because most people need to leave in order to seek therapy.

## SCENARIO 10

## "WE'RE LIKE A FAMILY"

***Corporate Speak:*** "We're like a family around here."
***Translation:*** "We pass down generational trauma to each other."

I believe part of my job as the Translator is to shame people for using absurdities until they no longer use them. Luckily, I feel we are almost at that point with this saying.

In any case—this is an all-time red flag in any job interview. Companies are not families. They are a business. They need to make business decisions, not familial decisions. Any self-respecting business will be transparent about that.

By saying "We're like a family around here," they are essentially saying that management feigns compassion for their employees but will still take advantage of them and drop them in the blink of an eye if they ever need to. That is far more manipulative. You can all still like one another while acknowledging that you're only hanging out because you are contractually obligated to, from nine to five, Monday through Friday. Both of those things can be true.

Make them provide examples of certain ways in which employees are treated like "family."

"Do you have an example of a situation in which human compassion was chosen over business value?"

If they can provide examples, then great. If not, big ol' red flag.

## SCENARIO 11

## YOU ARE A REPLACEMENT FOR AN EXISTING EMPLOYEE

***Corporate Speak:*** "You'll be replacing someone currently in seat."
***Translation:*** "We're stabbing someone in the back and will probably do the same to you."

This dynamic is similar to when you start a relationship with someone while they are in a relationship with someone else. If they cheat on their partner, odds are they will be willing to cheat on you. This is the corporate version of that.

If someone is being "transitioned out," you need to understand *why*. What went wrong? Why didn't it work out? Make them tell you the story so you can figure out whether you're about to step into the exact same mess.

And remember—being "transitioned out" doesn't always mean this person is about to be fired. Sometimes they are leaving on their own or it's a mutual split. In any case, you should ask to speak with that person—or at least someone who worked closely with them. If neither is an option, that usually means they're hiding something.

These conversations matter. They help you understand whether you'll be a better fit . . . or if you're walking straight into the same fate.

## SCENARIO 12

## THE COMPETITIVE ROLE

***Corporate Speak:*** "We have a number of candidates. This is highly competitive."

***Translation:*** "We are going to lowball you on salary."

This is used in a couple of scenarios and is a very common negotiating tactic. Put simply: They like you for the role but need to make you feel like they could give this job to anybody. All desirable jobs (even undesirable ones) should be competitive at all times, so it's unnecessary to point that out.

This phrase essentially says, "We have a number of candidates who are technically qualified, so we'll be giving it to the lowest bidder." Which, maybe they won't, but they want you to *think* they will.

Here's a great question to ask:

"I figured there would be other candidates. What are some of the key characteristics and experience that you're looking for in a candidate that would help someone push to the front of the pack?"

It will help you understand what a perfect fit looks like to them and, more important, if you are that perfect fit.

## SCENARIO 13

# "TAKE THIS BACK TO LEADERSHIP"

***Corporate Speak:*** "I'm going to take my thoughts back to leadership, and we'll be in touch."

***Translation:*** "You didn't get the job."

If an employer really likes you for the job, they are generally pretty open about that. Let's play out this scenario:

You ask, "What are the next steps from here?"

They respond, "I'm going to take my thoughts back to the team, and we'll be in touch." Spoiler: They are not going to be in touch. This is typically a way for them to ease you into rejection.

"It's not me who doesn't like you; it was my boss! These things go over my head!"

If someone really likes you, they are generally transparent about that and will openly discuss next steps. Sometimes there are HR guidelines to keep them from divulging too much, but generally if they need to "take it back to the team," their mind is made up.

Here's a way to navigate this part of the conversation:

**INTERVIEWER:** I'm going to circle back with the team to gather feedback, and we'll be in touch.

**YOU:** Totally understand there's internal deliberation. How do you think I'm stacking up against the other candidates you've spoken to?

**INTERVIEWER:** We have HR guidelines that prevent me from sharing too much.

Or:

**INTERVIEWER:** Yeah, that's what we still need to discuss.

*Translation:* You're cooked.

But sometimes you'll get something more promising:

**INTERVIEWER:** Honestly, I really like you. I just need to see how the others feel.

**YOU:** Got it. What's going to matter most to them? I want to understand whether the things you value in me will matter to them as well.

The point here is simple: Get a realistic read on where you stand, uncover any objections before they sink you, and either address them—or accept your fate and move on.

## SCENARIO 14

## MOVE FAST!!

*Corporate Speak:* "We're going to move very fast on this."
*Translation:* "We are prone to making bad decisions."

*BONUS Translation:* They are not going to move fast.

A company that claims to "move fast" usually just means they don't put in the level of thought and consideration required to make important decisions. They know that they need something and then railroad in a solution without vetting whether it's the *actual correct* decision.

***BONUS Translation:*** Congrats! You've been reading this book long enough that you've hit the daily double! Sometimes organizations say they move fast to get you to prioritize the job. In actuality, oftentimes they intentionally drag out the hiring process to get as many candidates in the door as possible. This allows them to keep you on the hook while giving the illusion that their decision will come soon.

Remember: You're vetting them just as much as they're vetting you. If they claim they "move fast," get a concrete outline of the hiring process and the exact timeline for each step. If they don't stick to it, that's a sign of internal dysfunction.

And if they really *are* ready to hire you immediately, treat it as a yellow flag. Either they're willing to hire anyone with a pulse, or you're wildly overqualified for what they actually need.

***BONUS Scenario:*** Sometimes "moving fast" is just a tactic to get you hyped. Suddenly you start prioritizing this role over others because it feels like low-hanging fruit. You'll think: *Wait, I don't have to survive a four-month gauntlet of interviews, decks, and homework? Sign me up!*

It's tempting—but don't bite. I've seen companies promise to "expedite" someone through the process only to pull a last-minute switch and announce they're choosing another candidate who, purely by coincidence, turns out to be the CEO's son-in-law.

## SCENARIO 15

# WISH THIS WAS FILLED YESTERDAY

***Corporate Speak:*** "We needed this role filled, like, yesterday, LOL."
***Translation:*** "Someone, or several people, quit unexpectedly."

Yesterday (or during some time frame in the near past), people quit, and the employer wishes they had been more prepared. When they tell you the role "should've been filled a long time ago," they're handing you a yellow flag. If it was so urgent, why didn't they fill it?

It usually means one of two things:

A) Several people left unexpectedly (voluntarily or not), and the team was caught flat-footed.

B) They've been neglecting this part of the business, letting the role go from a minor sore to a full-blown tumor.

Either way, it is worth digging into.

# STARTING A NEW JOB

The best part of starting a new job is being sent off into a sea of PDFs, Word docs, PowerPoint presentations, and employees telling you to "reach out if you need anything," and then not answering your Slack messages when you do.

One time I joined a client on their first day at a new job. This is how their first meeting with HR went:

**HR:** Welcome to the team! The first step will be to get your systems all set up.
**REP:** Okay, great, and who should I go to for help with that?
**HR:** Um, I believe it's Mark, but let me check.
**TRANSLATOR:** She doesn't know.

It's very important to vet out training and enablement resources during the interview process. But let's say you didn't, and you have no idea what you're walking into. Read on for a few common onboarding programs.

SCENARIO 1

## THE "COMPREHENSIVE" PROGRAM

***Corporate Speak:*** "We have a robust onboarding program to get you up to speed."

***Translation:*** "We have a Google document and a slide deck with a bunch of random information that hasn't been updated since 2019."

Traditionally, a "robust" onboarding program means that someone at some point in the company's distant past threw together a bundle of files you're now expected to memorize because they're the *only* support you'll get. It's a convenient way for the company to dodge the actual time and responsibility required to help someone understand the product, the market, and, frankly, what the hell is going on.

Usually this "packet" gets updated once every six years and is an incredibly ineffective way to learn anything. You'll have perfectly normal questions, only to be told, "It's in the onboarding document." You will then spend forty-five minutes hunting for a simple answer buried on page 87 of a PDF that was created during the Obama administration.

The key is to not treat the "comprehensive" packet as gospel. Sure, documents and decks can be helpful for basic context, but real learning happens through asking questions, observing situations, and talking to actual humans. That's where you pick up the nuances you'll never get from a static slide.

And speaking of static—these packets are almost never updated. The world changes faster than any company's ability (or willingness) to revise a PowerPoint. If something is written in a "company bible," you can assume it was accurate for about five minutes after it was created. So skim it for the useful kernels, but rely on the knowledge and experiences of the people around you to understand the real landscape.

## SCENARIO 2

## THE "THRIVE IN AMBIGUITY" PROGRAM

***Corporate Speak:*** "We need our new hires to thrive in ambiguity."
***Translation:*** "We don't have an onboarding program, so just go figure it out."

If you ever ask a company what their onboarding program looks like and they say, "We're looking for people who can thrive in ambiguity," just know that *you are* the onboarding program. You'll be given system logins, a meeting with each department one time, and then be expected to be good at the job within three months. You'll have to be proactive and learn things on your own, while everyone who works there is likely too burned out to help you.

If you find yourself in this situation, it's important to understand that no one is coming to help—you need to make help happen. They're relying on you to figure it out. You must be outgoing, proactive, and aggressive about your own learning. Don't sit on your hands, waiting for someone to "throw time on your calendar." *You* reach out—*you* put time on *their* calendar.

"Thrive in ambiguity" is Corporate Speak for "We need someone who can succeed when there are no answers." You're now responsible for figuring out the questions, finding the answers, and building your own process. It requires an extra level of proactivity and assertiveness to make it work. If you can't do that, failure is likely. Worth mentioning—you might be destined for failure anyway. ¯_(ツ)_/¯

## SCENARIO 3

## THE "DRINK THE KOOL-AID" PROGRAM

***Corporate Speak:*** "Our culture is everything, so we designed an onboarding program that will get you fully bought in and up to speed."

***Translation:*** "ONE OF US. ONE OF US. ONE OF US."

While "Drink the Kool-Aid" (page 47) programs are often genuinely helpful and thorough, they also seem less like a training program and more like a baptism into a new cult. You can look forward to a large amount of documentation, a nauseating number of presentations, and one-on-ones with every person at the organization who has consumed the juice. And anyone who hasn't? The business will intentionally hide these people from you.

If you're someone who needs structure and guidance, this is a great fit. If you are someone who "thrives in ambiguity," it might be frustrating. In either case, it's always important to avoid the "groupthink." Think critically, understand the problems, and make sure the Kool-Aid isn't laced with something.

## Corporate Translation

# THE NONSENSE EMAIL

Everybody's been there–you get an email with a daunting subject line from your boss that you already know is going to suck and probably won't make much sense. It's a fear tactic and also part of the documentation process in case things in the organization go south. Typically, it looks something like this:

**EXAMPLE**

**Subject Line: Aligning on Q2 Priorities**

Hi, [Name],

As we enter a make-or-break quarter, it's critical that our efforts are fully aligned to our OKRs and focused on delivering measurable impact. The success of this quarter will set the trajectory for the rest of the year, so executing at maximized efficiency is essential.

I'd like you to take ownership of the high-priority initiatives in your area, proactively identifying blockers, coordinating with stakeholders, and driving actionable solutions. Monitor KPIs closely to track performance, measure progress against our OKRs, and course-correct proactively as needed.

Please come prepared for a sync next week with a concise update on initiatives, key milestones, potential risks, and opportunities to accelerate impact. Your contributions are pivotal to hitting our KPIs, achieving our OKRs, and ensuring the organization stays on track for success.

Best regards,
Goober McBossBoss
SVP of Strategic Alignment

## TRANSLATION

**Subject Line: Do your job or we are screwed!!**

Hi, [Name],

It's a make-or-break quarter, and yes, I know I say that every quarter–but I actually mean it this time (no, I don't). We have goals, and if we don't hit them, my life will be a living hell for the rest of the year as we play catch-up. And because of that, I will inevitably make your life a living hell, too.

I need you to do your job really well by fixing problems, coordinating with whoever else needs to be involved, and making sure our stuff gets done on time. Please also micromanage the team, and if anything looks off for more than twenty minutes, you should yell at somebody.

We'll sync next week, and you better know how things are tracking–and if they're not tracking, have a plan to fix it. I know a lot of this is technically my job, but I'm just going to put it all on you!!! Don't screw up!

Best regards,
Goober McBossBoss
SVP of Strategic Alignment

# PERFORMANCE REVIEWS

Every year, performance review season is an exhausting time in the life of the Corporate Translator. The amount of Corporate Speak companies will spew to avoid giving raises or honest feedback is truly remarkable (horrifying). Jargon is deliberately used to create confusion, leaving people with no idea what just happened—or where they stand with the company. Which means I have to work overtime.

For example, I was once called into a performance review conducted for a lower-level employee who had been a consistent top performer for two years. Her "quarterly performance review" happened only once every nine months and lacked any real substance. The first fifteen minutes were spent on meaningless small talk, the next fourteen on gossip about the company, and the final minute asking if there was anything she needed.

She responded:

> "Yeah, actually. I've been here for two years and would like to know what my next step at the company is."

Only to be met with:

> "Oh, sorry—looks like we're out of time! Let's pick this back up in our next conversation."

***Translator:*** "We are intentionally deflecting you and hope that you won't bring this up again."

This is an intentional strategy designed to keep you stuck indefinitely. After all, top performers can't remain top performers if they dare to take on new roles, new skills, or career progression. The nerve of them to want to grow!

Generally, there are three key strategies used to deliver feedback to top performers, average performers, and underperformers. Let's look at each so you can determine where you stand.

## SCENARIO 1

## NO FEEDBACK

***Corporate Speak:*** "Honestly, I don't have a ton of feedback for you."

***Translation:*** "You are amazing at your job, and we don't want you to know how much we can't lose you."

Sometimes in corporate, saying nothing is saying something. In this case, they said nothing while saying something—and somehow also said a lot at the same time. Make sense? Of course it doesn't.

If you're in good standing with the organization, praise is usually given publicly, while private recognition is limited. Why? Because public praise makes everyone clap, you feel good, and ideally you bask in that moment without pushing for your actual worth. But if they praise you privately, suddenly the door opens for you to ****gasp**** ask for a raise! How dare you!

If you find yourself in this scenario, you need to advocate for yourself. Even if you have a manager who is willing to listen, they still have to fight *their* manager, who then has to fight *their* manager, and so on. The point is: Operate under the assumption that no one is coming to save you—you have to save yourself. Don't let them waste time or dance around the conversation. Make them discuss a real path forward with clearly defined steps. Or take the simpler route: Get another offer and watch them squeal.

## SCENARIO 2

## "TIGHTEN THINGS UP"

***Corporate Speak:*** "You're doing well, with a few things that need to be tightened up."

***Translation:*** "You're completely average. Please stop being average."

Phrases like "Tighten up" or "Take things to the next level" are often used on average performers that the company would like to elevate to above-average performers (but still want to pay like average performers).

If you find yourself in Scenario 2, make the business offer proper incentives. People normally stay average for extended periods of time only because they are not properly incentivized. You should be willing and happy to increase your performance so long as your efforts are met with a proportional increase in your wallet.

## SCENARIO 3

# PIP OR PRE-PIP

***Corporate Speak:*** "I believe in you, and that's why I know you're capable of so much more."

***Translation:*** "I don't like you and am already preparing to get rid of you."

"We believe in you" is Corporate Speak for "We are losing faith in you by the second." This is very common groundwork for companies to lay down for a PIP or pre-PIP conversations.

If you find yourself in Scenario 3, they've already had PIP (see page 51) conversations about you behind your back. That is a very deep hole to dig yourself out of. You either need to start stepping up (work harder) or start stepping out (apply to jobs harder).

# RAISE AND PROMOTIONAL CONVERSATIONS (REJECTIONS)

The mental gymnastics companies perform to avoid paying and promoting people tend to keep a Corporate Translator like me on the metaphorical balance beam all year long. One time I had someone who hadn't received a raise in three years ask me to sit in on his one-on-one with his manager as he requested one. The conversation went like this:

**REP:** I've been here for three years, the cost of living has skyrocketed, and I've been a consistent performer my entire tenure.

**MANAGER:** I hear you. The problem is we're strapped for cash right now, and all raise conversations are on hold until we land additional funding.

**REP:** Okay . . . and when will that be?

**MANAGER:** TBD (see page 55).

**TRANSLATOR:** Sometime between a few months from now and never.

It would be nice to live in a perfect world where meritocracy prevails and people who earn recognition actually receive it. Unfortunately, this is not a perfect world, a meritocracy, or even a rational environment—it's corporate. Read on for some of the most common tactics companies use to avoid paying you what you're worth and tips on how to handle each one.

## SCENARIO 1

# BLAMING THE BUDGET

*Corporate Speak:* "Budgets are tight."
*Translation:* "We don't want to spend our money on you."

Of all the organizations I've ever translated for, every single one had a "tight" budget. I have never encountered a company that was like, "Hey, ya know what? We actually do have a bunch of money, so I'm glad you asked for some of it." Not even once. It's almost as if they *do* have money but are just very picky about where they allocate it.

In this situation, typically your best course of action is to go get another offer. Even if you conduct market analysis and do in-depth presentations on how good of a performer you are, you are still going to be fighting for scraps. I've seen it happen countless times: Organizations "don't have the budget," but as soon as they are in a position where they are about to lose a good employee, the budget magically appears.

## SCENARIO 2

# THE "STRING ALONG"

*Corporate Speak:* "We'd like to see you thrive in this role a little longer."
*Translation:* "We want to kick this can down the road in six-month increments until you either quit or stop asking."

Kicking the can down the road is one of corporate's favorite tactics. As a Translator, it works in my favor since I charge per meeting—recycling the same conversation every six months ensures a steady cash flow. The goal of this method is to bleed you dry. They realize that if they push things out in increments, they can just delay your raise all the way to retirement.

It's reasonable for an employer to ask you to demonstrate strong performance for an extended period of time—but you need them to commit to a specific time frame and clear metrics. It cannot be a vague, noncommittal "Just do better for longer." Make them give you clearly defined targets you need to hit in order to earn it (even if you've already met them).

## SCENARIO 3

## "WE CAN'T GIVE EVERYONE A RAISE"

***Corporate Speak:*** "If we give you a raise, then we need to give everyone a raise."

***Translation:*** "Please shut up."

I've heard this one a good amount, and it's quite the doozy! The ol' "Well, if we give you a raise, then everyone's going to want a raise" is a real classic. But . . . this is *your* performance review. Why is your boss talking about other people?

This is where you need to come prepared to make the case for yourself. Beat them at their own game by providing "data-driven insights" that show why you stand out from the crowd. It's not about other employees or even market rates—it's about *your* value to the company, which is defined by your contributions. Come with a presentation that highlights the key metrics you've achieved and the opportunity cost of losing someone like you.

# TEAM MEETINGS

"Groupthink" is when a group prioritizes agreement with the consensus over critical thinking, causing people to suppress their doubts. The corporate version of this is "group-confusion," which is when a group hears a barrage of confusing buzzwords and collectively shrugs and forgets about it because no one wants to strain their brain. That's what a lot of team meetings turn into: One person at the front speaks nonsense while the rest of the team stares at one another in total bewilderment, and then the meeting ends. Luckily, the Corporate Translator exists to help make sense of these meetings. Let's dive into some common scenarios.

My job is very often to translate from the manager to their direct report. However, some of my favorite jobs have been when lower-level employees bring me to translate on their behalf. As an example, one time I got called in to translate because one leader in the organization would say a bunch of nonsense words, ask if everyone was "tracking," and then take their collective silence as a yes. Every meeting looked like this:

**MANAGER:** We need to optimize our deliverables and drive execution across our strategic alignments. Are we all on the same page?
**EMPLOYEES:** *collective bewilderment*
**TRANSLATOR:** No.

Let's look at some of the most common meeting scenarios.

## SCENARIO 1

# CIRCLING THE WAGONS OF SHAME

***Corporate Speak:*** "Just circling the wagons to see how we are tracking on our action items."

***Translation:*** "Let's publicly shame people who are behind on their goals."

This scenario is very similar to when your teacher collected homework one by one. They'd stop at the one or two people who didn't have it, listen to their excuse, mutter something in disdain, and keep moving. The adult version? Go around the room, individually handing out either accolades or criticism:

"Good job."

"Good job."

"SHAME."

"SHAME."

"Good job."

Everyone leaves vaguely embarrassed or mildly relieved and no more productive than when they walked in.

A good way to handle these situations is to stop focusing on what went wrong and start focusing on how to fix it. If someone is going to be publicly called out for falling behind, it should also be a group effort to help them solve it. These meetings would be much better served to have a collaborative effort over what is working for people and how the recipe can be adopted across the team. Uncover obstacles and ideate on how to solve them instead of assuming people are behind because they want to be.

## SCENARIO

## THE "COULD'VE BEEN AN EMAIL" MEETING

***Corporate Speak:*** "Hey, guys, just wanted to do a quick touch base on . . ."

***Translation:*** "This message could've been transmitted via any form of digital communication, but I prefer to waste time in person."

If it's a "touch base" (see page 26), it doesn't need to be blocked off on your calendar. Tell them you're busy and would like to know the agenda. If it is something important and an in-person discussion is necessary or required, then that should be communicated.

## SCENARIO 3

## THE TEAM UPDATE

***Corporate Speak:*** "Hey, all, just throwing time on your calendars for a quick team update."

***Translation:*** "Someone got canned."

Anytime you see a fifteen-minute full-team block pop up on your calendar involving any combination of "team" and "update," someone's been fired. Employers do this so they can ask, "Does anyone have any questions or concerns?" and then wait for people to look around at one another befuddled, not wanting to speak. They then say, "Okay, well, if anyone wants to talk offline, I'm around."

Spoiler: They are not around.

Ideally, this information should not have caught you off guard. If it did, it's okay to ask questions to understand what went wrong. While they might not owe it to you, any employer that actually cares about how their employees feel will want that level of communication with you.

## SCENARIO 4

## POST-ELT FREAK-OUT SESSION

***Corporate Speak:*** "We need to meet right away to discuss our KPI tracking."

***Translation:*** "Middle management just got yelled at by upper management, and you are about to be severely micromanaged."

It's always an exciting time in a Translator's life when middle management has to meet with upper management—usually on a monthly basis. They never come out of those meetings thinking, *Okay, nothing to discuss.* Instead, they emerge stressed to the gills, ready to micromanage everyone, and eager to call a stand-up meeting to tell everyone how screwed they are via a bunch of corporate buzzwords.

These meetings are like walking into a blender full of panic, stress, and confusion. Why? Because your manager *is* a walking blender of panic, stress, and confusion—and will probably try to fix it with a literal cocktail after they sign off. Naturally, that chaos spills onto the rest of the team. It's basically Mom and/or Dad coming home in a bad mood and instantly infecting the whole house with doom energy.

Here's the thing: That stress is theirs, not yours. Your job is to mentally slap on noise-canceling headphones, compartmentalize, and only take action on the stuff you can actually control. If there's something actionable you can do to improve, go ahead and do it. If it's just stress for stress's sake . . . congratulations! Welcome to life under this particular manager. It's not a fun ride. Grab your popcorn and enjoy the roller coaster. Well, I guess you wouldn't eat popcorn on a roller coaster, but . . . you get it.

## SCENARIO 5
## THE PIVOT

***Corporate Speak:*** "Hey, team, we're currently working on pivoting priorities."

***Translation:*** "We realized that everything we've told you for the past three months is wrong."

Corporate LOVES a pivot. They pivot so often that I'm not sure they even know what direction is north or south anymore. It's very similar to a corporate version of *The Blair Witch Project.* (For any younger readers, *The Blair Witch Project* is a movie about a group of friends who go camping in the woods, get lost, and are subsequently stalked by a witch.)

The "Blair Witch" in this scenario is layoffs. Management pivots too many times, winds up completely lost, and the witch lurks . . . and you know who *doesn't* love a pivot? Everyone who actually has to do the work. They are basically told, "Hey, just stop doing what you're doing even though we told you to do it, and now do something completely different, and if it doesn't work out, you'll likely get fired." Fun stuff!

While it's important to be *agile* (see page 18), it's equally important to have direction. Constantly getting pulled in new directions turns your team into a bunch of squirrels chasing every nut in sight.

Ask critical questions:

- "Why are we moving away from the previous direction?"
- "Why are we confident this new direction will yield better results?"
- "Why has this suddenly become a higher priority?"

If you don't understand the reasoning behind these pivots, you'll keep getting pulled in every direction—and eventually you'll end up in a haunted house in the middle of the woods while your friends are being taken by a witch . . . metaphorically, of course.

# COMPANY ANNOUNCEMENTS

Company announcements can elicit a wide range of emotions, such as stress, joy, confusion, happiness, anger, stress again, and so on. The one thing they will have in common? Nothing will be transparent.

I'm very often called into all-hands meetings. It's virtually impossible for leadership to be fully honest with the entire company at once, which makes these meetings ripe for Corporate Speak—and drama.

One time, I was called into a mandatory all-hands meeting that went like this:

**CEO:** We received feedback that company morale is low.

**TRANSLATOR:** They decided to *actually* listen to their employees.

**CEO:** Thanks for that, Translator. As a result, we're going to hold a quarterly on-site meeting for the entire company to facilitate collaboration.

**TRANSLATOR:** Never mind. No, they didn't.

Nonetheless, company announcements are always an exciting time. Let's look at some of the most common scenarios.

## SCENARIO 1

# LEADERSHIP CHANGE

***Corporate Speak:*** "[XYZ person] will be transitioning out of the company. We really appreciate their contributions and are excited for their next journey."

***Translation:*** "This leader has been forced out."

Whenever a leadership change is announced, it's always made to sound like some nice, amicable, considerate parting of ways when, in actuality, it was likely months of arguing behind the scenes. Here are emojis to illustrate this principle:

Announcement: 😊😃🥳
Behind the Scenes: 😡🤬😠

"Transitioning," "leaving," "parting ways"—they're all polite ways of saying "We fired this person but gave them a nice severance package." The only real joy and gratitude these people feel in this situation is that they no longer have to work together.

## SCENARIO 2

# LAYOFFS

***Corporate Speak:*** "We're doing some organizational restructuring in order to become more lean."

***Translation:*** "Things aren't going well, and we had to get rid of a bunch of people."

Honestly, layoffs didn't used to be a huge part of my job as a Translator. Communications on this subject used to be pretty straightforward: "Hey, our business isn't doing well, and we need to cut expenses."

But now, layoffs have become so common that there are countless reasons why they might happen. Companies will raise massive rounds of funding and immediately lay people off. They'll have record-breaking years and still lay people off. The list goes on. It's become strange, watching layoffs evolve from a clear negative to something organizations try to spin as a positive.

"We had to lay people off—and here's why that's actually a good thing."

Yes, that is now a real and common conversation.

"We're becoming more lean."

"We're driving operational efficiency."

"We're restructuring to optimize the business."

Here's a plea from the Corporate Translator to companies who prefer this kind of phrasing: Please—just say, "Some things weren't working, and we had to reevaluate parts of the business to make changes." Most employees simply want some real honesty instead of being told everything is great while a large portion of their colleagues are being shown the door.

The reality is, most companies overhire based on inflated projections (that they don't hit), and then they have to cut the workforce. That's a hard conversation to have—which is precisely why I exist.

If you're one of the lucky ones who survived—good news! Your job is now 100 percent safe forever.

I'm kidding. Obviously.

In reality, layoffs usually signal one of two things: serious financial turbulence or a major restructuring of how the business plans to operate going forward. Your job is *not* to pretend this is a "necessary step for future success" or whatever PR-friendly line they feed you. Your job is to understand *why* the layoffs happened so you can gauge whether the future is going to look any different than the past.

Don't let leadership sweet-talk you into believing this is somehow a good thing. Make them explain exactly what went wrong, why it's happening now, and—most important—what they're changing to ensure you're not sitting through another round of this in six months.

## SCENARIO 2.5:
## THE REORG

***Corporate Speak:*** "This reorg will allow us to align to our long-term vision."

***Translation:*** "Some people got fired, and the remaining people will be squeezed dry."

Reorgs are the sibling of layoffs—the slightly more polite but equally chaotic one. As mentioned earlier, layoffs usually signal one of two things: serious financial turbulence or a major restructuring of how the business plans to operate. A reorg is the latter.

It means leadership realized they had the wrong process, wrong strategy, wrong people, wrong financial models—basically wrong *everything*. So a bunch of people got fired under the pleasant umbrella of "strategic alignment." The reorg is their attempt to wipe the slate clean and start fresh.

For the people who survive the purge, the chaos usually gets worse. Everyone suddenly has a new job (or two, or three), reports to new people, has new targets, and is expected to pretend they know what's going on. Spoiler: No one does.

If you find yourself in the middle of a reorg, follow the same playbook as with layoffs: Understand *why* it's happening, what's changing, and why leadership believes this time will magically be different. If your role or responsibilities have changed, clarify what they are, who you now report to, and what your targets look like.

And if the new role is something you can't stomach, it may be time to "reorg" yourself . . . right out of the org.

## SCENARIO 3

## THE ACQUISITION

***Corporate Speak:*** "We're excited to announce our new strategic partners."

***Translation:*** "Someone just bought the company, and it's going to be a sh*t show."

Acquisitions are like a cousin to layoffs and reorganizations. Technically, they're not the same thing—but if we're being honest, they kind of are. They typically happen for one of two main reasons:

1. The company isn't performing well enough to move toward an IPO or raise another major round of funding, but it's doing just well enough that new investors believe they can fix it.
2. A bigger fish wanted to scoop it up.

The reason acquisitions still fall within the layoff family is because they typically follow the same pattern: "We're very excited to announce this partnership! Oh, and by the way, it's going to come with workforce reductions, leadership changes, and restructuring—but it's an exciting time for us!"

Here's what they won't tell you: If it's an "exciting time" for *them*, it's probably not going to be an exciting time for *you*. They'll position it as a positive—and technically it is. Maybe it saved the company from going under or enabled a massive overnight expansion.

But it also brings the same destructive chaos you'd expect from a reorg. If you're in a good place at the company and genuinely believe in the new direction, great—ride it out. If not, it might be the perfect time to cash in your equity (all .0000000001 percent of it).

## SCENARIO 4

## THE ALL-HANDS SPEECH

***Corporate Speak:*** "We had a great quarter. I couldn't be more proud of this team."

***Translation:*** "We had a great quarter. None of you will see the benefits of that."

The all-hands speech could keep me busy for a week. It's basically a way to tell everyone that they're doing great work, the company is doing well, and they will definitely not benefit from that at all. Employees can keep working in their same positions for the same wage, but thanks for the effort!

The reality is the company is probably not doing *that* well. The all-hands meetings are designed to highlight all the positives and hide or gloss over the negatives. The difference between what's said publicly and what happens behind the scenes could be an entire sketch comedy routine.

The quarter is usually full of stressed leaders pointing fingers at each other in the boardroom—and then standing in front of the company, talking about how much they appreciate their "rock star colleagues."

People get shout-outs they don't deserve. Numbers are cherry-picked. Real issues never get discussed. It's essentially the corporate version of the show *Whose Line Is It Anyway?*—nothing makes sense, and the numbers are made up.

Take all-hands meetings for what they are: a corporate high school pep rally. Everyone gets together to pump their fists, shake some metaphorical pom-poms, and watch the CEO do a symbolic cartwheel. They are almost never a real indicator of the company's financial or cultural health.

## SCENARIO 5

# THE COMPANY SURVEY

***Corporate Speak:*** "We really value your perspective and appreciate candid feedback."

***Translation:*** "We'd like to collect your feedback so that we can do nothing with it."

The company survey is one of the most valuable tools in the entire corporate gaslighting arsenal. What better way to make people feel "heard" than a completely "anonymous" survey with ideas on how to improve operations?

It's a great way to allow people to vent without actually being able to vent. There are no productive conversations happening, simply a few forms that will get jumbled together and tossed in the digital trash.

It's all obligatory questions like:

*How satisfied are you with your job?*
*Do you feel you are in a position to succeed?*
*Would you recommend that a friend work here?*
*Are you compensated fairly?*

All of those are multiple-choice options so that they can average them out and do nothing with the information. The *best* part is that, oftentimes, they will actually make a change based on employee feedback, but it'll be a change that no one really asked for.

So, there will be an announcement that says, "Good news! We took the results of the survey and decided to make some changes.

Fifty-five percent of you stated that you don't see a career path, so we're offering a $50 voucher for a training course of your choosing! We hear you!!!"

Meanwhile, 90 percent of the company responded that they don't have confidence in the direction of leadership, but that one will be shrugged off as an "algorithm error."

You can still use the surveys to voice your frustrations, but just know that they are:

A) Definitely not anonymous
B) Very unlikely to result in meaningful change

## SCENARIO 6

## THE "NEW TOOL" ANNOUNCEMENT

***Corporate Speak:*** "Our executive leadership decided to make a substantial investment in a solution that will drive operational efficiency."

***Translation:*** "Here's a new tool that will be a major disruption to your lives and that no one will learn how to use."

Ah, the classic: "Here's a new tool that you all need to learn, and we promise it's better than the last one that everyone hated!"

For months, without the knowledge of the people who will actually use it, the executive team has been evaluating a "solution" that was promised to revolutionize the organization. Most of the employees who will be impacted by the tool were barely involved in the discussion. At best, they sat through a demo call with their cameras off, catching up on emails.

Leadership then railroads the new tool into place, forcing everyone to figure it out while insisting they did it for their benefit. In reality, the CEO's brother-in-law is a VP of sales for the vendor and offered a "friends and family" discount.

It's important to remember that at some point in your career, this will inevitably happen. It's always in your best interest to learn new technologies—even when they're inefficient or counterproductive. Sometimes life hands you a lemon, and that lemon is an overpriced software tool that adds very little value to your day-to-day.

## SCENARIO 7

## THE REBRAND

***Corporate Speak:*** "We're excited to announce a sleek new look on our company's brand."

***Translation:*** "We have a new website and slide deck."

Rebrands are almost always led by new marketing leaders who come in promising to bring the company into "the new age." In reality, this usually just means an updated website and a new slide-deck template. That's pretty much it.

The company gathers, rings the bell, and celebrates like it's some momentous milestone in the organization's history—when, in reality, nothing materially changes.

## SCENARIO 8

# THE "COMPANY VALUES" REFRESHER

***Corporate Speak:*** "It's time for us to realign our company's core values."

***Translation:*** "Let's revisit the values that no one in the company upholds."

Company values are always very cringe. They are normally the same random collection of adjectives packaged up into a neat acronym. Let's look at an example:

*Here at Obligatory Tech Corp, our employees commit to being NUMB:*

***N**ice*
***U**nderstanding*
***M**otivated*
***B**old*

*Everyone who works here is NUMB. If you're not NUMB, you are simply not going to fit in!*

Every six months or so, the company will get everyone back together to remind them why they should be NUMB.

## SCENARIO 9

# PRODUCT LAUNCH

***Corporate Speak:*** "This new feature will be an absolute game changer in the space."

***Translation:*** "We were supposed to have this eighteen months ago."

They throw around terms like *revolutionary*, *game-changing*, and *innovative* when, realistically, no one feature is going to do that (or if it does, it's exceedingly rare). New features are very often pushed out in a rush because the competition already has them and the company feels behind. And the best part? They'll likely be half-baked or full of bugs for six to eight months! Fun stuff!

It's always important to understand *why* these developments were made. Of all the ways to use our developers' time, why *this*?

"Are we the first to market with this feature?"

"Did the lack of it actually cost us deals?"

"How will this materially impact revenue?"

Don't get lost in the hype. Always dig into the why behind a product innovation to figure out whether it's actually worth celebrating.

# HR AND PEOPLE OPERATIONS

Of all the departments, Human Resources is probably the one that keeps me busiest as a Translator. They overuse Corporate Speak words more than almost any other department—which is ironic, considering they're supposed to be the "open communication and transparency" team. Most of the time, they have to speak a certain way to avoid potential litigation, but sometimes I think it's because they actually enjoy it.

One time, I was emergency-added to a client's one-on-one with his manager because he noticed that HR was added to the invite. This is how it went:

**MANAGER:** I added HR as a resource for this conversation.

**HR:** Yes, and first off, we just wanted to let you know that you're not getting fired.

**TRANSLATOR:** Yet.

**HR:** We just feel like your performance has slipped these past few months and want to understand what's going on.

**TRANSLATOR:** You're getting PIP'd.

Never forget: HR is employed by the company, not by you. Let's take a look at some of the most common HR interactions.

## SCENARIO 1

# WE'RE HIRING

***Corporate Speak:*** "We're growing rapidly and looking to scale the team!"

***Translation:*** "We need to show we're hiring in order to appease investors."

Generally, companies only "scale fast" for two main reasons:

A) They recently got funding.

B) They desperately need funding.

In either case, it normally ends poorly. Instead of taking a tactful, systematic approach to hiring, they'll just hire far too many people in a very short period of time. This provides the illusion that the company is "exploding 🚀🚀🦄🦄🦄 with unlimited potential!" Whether the financials of the company actually support that is irrelevant.

Rapid hiring is very commonly followed by rapid firing. There's no consideration for consequences, just "we need to scale, so hopefully we can add a lot of people and it works out."

Spoiler: A lot of the time, it doesn't work out. They grow the cup first, hoping there's enough water to fill it. Then, they fall short of expectations (the water) and need to *rightsize* the cup (see page 42). That's why it's important to understand the justification behind the hiring. Will it be sustainable, or will the huge initial burst inevitably lead to an even bigger crash?

SCENARIO 2

## WE'RE NOT HIRING

*Corporate Speak:* "We've decided to put a temporary pause on hiring."

*Translation:* "We're hemorrhaging money!"

Generally, healthy companies should always be hiring. People are always leaving, and there should always be some kind of need somewhere in the business.

So if your company suddenly shouts, "Okay, game sealed!" that's usually the first sign of trouble. It means the cash isn't cashing. Finances are in such rough shape that they can't even stomach bringing on one more salary.

This is typically a precursor to layoffs:

**"We're hiring!" → "We're not hiring!" → "We're firing!"**

This is always a very large red flag. It's normal for a company to not be in HOCKEY STICK GROWTH mode all the time. However, if higher-ups were recently excited about all the openings in the company and then all of a sudden just went "Whoops, never mind," it means there is trouble.

## SCENARIO 3

# RTO ANNOUNCEMENT

***Corporate Speak:*** "We want to facilitate a collaborative environment."

***Translation:*** "We want to keep closer tabs on all of you."

There will be a million different justifications for why companies want people to return to the office, and all of them translate to "we want to keep an eye on you."

Collaboration, community, culture, productivity—they all ultimately mean *surveillance.*

Human interaction is genuinely valuable, but any reasonable company should be willing to allow flexibility in the name of employee well-being. In today's world, any employer with zero remote flexibility can't pretend it's for any reason other than micromanagement.

Unfortunately, there is not much you can do to stop it. Unless you want to try to get a doctor's note that you have a severe allergy to other humans. Might be worth a shot.

## SCENARIO 4

# THE EXIT INTERVIEW

***Corporate Speak:*** "We'd like to hear what we could do differently."

***Translation:*** "Nothing will change! Best of luck!!"

The exit interview is always attractive to employees who finally have a (perceived) platform to voice all their frustrations without any consequences.

It'll be cathartic for the soon-to-be ex-employee, feeling as though they will actually impact change since they no longer need to hold back. In reality, any critical feedback will be chalked up as a disgruntled employee's bias.

Take these conversations for what they are: an opportunity to voice all the pent-up frustrations you've built over your tenure, and an opportunity for them to pretend that things will change. Really, it's just a space to get things off your chest so that, hopefully, you don't leave a negative Glassdoor review. Nothing will change—and that's okay, because you're moving on to greener pastures anyway.

## SCENARIO 5

## THE CULTURE INITIATIVE

***Corporate Speak:*** "We're rolling out a key initiative to strengthen our culture."

***Translation:*** "You're going to do a bunch of activities that you don't want to do."

Companies will invest tens of thousands of dollars into team-building events to "strengthen culture" when, realistically, if they just gave employees that money, it would go much further toward improving happiness.

Culture initiatives often just force people into events they don't actually want to attend. People work a huge portion of their lives so they can support the things and people they love—not so they can spend another evening pretending to enjoy a corporate scavenger hunt.

Giving people raises or bonuses will almost always go further toward employee satisfaction than forcing everyone to participate in a murder-mystery event. That's my opinion, but what do I know? I'm just a local office service animal.

## SCENARIO 6
## THE CHECK-IN

***Corporate Speak:*** "Hey, just wanted to check in to see how things are going."

***Translation:*** "You might be 'cooked,' as the kids are saying nowadays."

Normally, if HR is doing random check-ins with you, leadership has been talking about you, and not in a good way. You are either underperforming or causing drama that they don't want to deal with.

HR "checking in" with you is the start of the documentation process. They will begin the conversation under the guise of "I just wanted to see how you're feeling," or whatever other justification they come up with, when really they are just trying to gauge if you are salvageable or not.

## SCENARIO 7

# THE COLLEAGUE FEEDBACK

*Corporate Speak:* "I'm just meeting with a few individuals to understand how your experience has been working with this person."

*Translation:* "We are trying to fire this person."

Most companies will attempt to gather some sort of paper trail prior to letting go of an employee. Congrats! If you hear the above, *you* are now the paper trail. If HR is going around looking for "feedback" about a certain person, it means their mind is made up and they just need the documented evidence to cover their a**.

Your level of participation is up to you—just know that your words can, and will, be used against someone else. For future reference, here is the corporate version of your Miranda rights:

> You have the right to remain silent.
> Anything you say can and will be used against your coworker.
> You have the right to an attorney.
> If you cannot afford one—too bad, we're not going to pay for it.
> You can decide at any time to exercise these rights and return to driving shareholder value.

Generally, I think it's best to stay out of office drama. But then . . . what's the point of even working? Just to *do work*?! Boring!

# PART 3

# CORPORATE TRANSLATOR TIPS

Now, I hesitated to write this section—because if I taught everyone how to navigate the Corporate Speak language, there would be no need for a Translator. And in today's alarmingly confusing workplace, my calendar is beyond full—I feel like Santa on Christmas Eve every day of my life. There's just way too much jargon and not enough me. Therefore, I feel somewhat justified in pointing you all in the right direction when it comes to navigating certain situations, and not just translating but getting to a place where real communication will happen.

There are three distinct parts in this section:

1. Operational Navigation Protocols (Navigational Tips to Protect from the Facade)
2. Strategic Mindset Enablement Framework (Adopt the Translator Mindset)
3. Action Items to Drive Adoption (How to Improve Workplace Communication)

# OPERATIONAL NAVIGATION PROTOCOLS

*(Navigational Tips to Protect from the Facade)*

You've encountered some Corporate Speak in the wild. What do you do? Do you phone a friend? Ask ChatGPT? Have a panic attack? Perhaps all three?

Don't worry; the Translator is here to help you manage these situations.

## TIP 1

## SAY IT BACK TO THEM

Example:

***Corporate Speak:*** "We really need to tighten this up."
***Response:*** "Just to be clear—when you say 'tighten things up,' what specific actions need to be changed, and what are some best practices we can follow?"

One of the main frustrations of Corporate Speak is the intentional vagueness. Instead of clearly defining the problem and outlining the specific actions needed to fix it, they just throw out some indistinct metaphor.

Make them "distinct" it. Speak their own words back to them and ask them to provide a more thorough explanation with clearly defined goals and outcomes that everyone must follow. It's management's job to offer guidance and a framework for how to improve (and succeed). The answer cannot be "Just do better." It is their job to delineate specific ways for people to improve along with a model for the team to follow.

## TIP 2

## MAKE THEM DEFINE IT

***Corporate Speak:*** "We can't give you a raise quite yet; we need to see you thrive in this role a little longer."

***Response:*** "Understood. What specific targets do I need to hit in what time frame in order to earn a raise?"

If your employer can't clearly define those, they are likely stringing you along. They should be able to say:

> "If you are above 90 percent of quota for the next six months, we will guarantee a raise of at least XYZ percent."

If you hear this, it means they are going to drag this process out as long as they can. It's Psychology 101: You dangle a carrot and tell the rabbit that if it achieves certain targets, it gets the carrot.

Unfortunately, the current corporate culture is full of undefined carrots. This is intentional—it allows them the freedom to do whatever they want. There used to be fixed targets: "If you're here for a year, you'll earn a 10 percent raise," etc. Merit-based raises? What a concept!

Now all the goals you must achieve are amorphous: "Just do good for an indefinite period of time." Do not settle for this. You are owed specific targets and the rewards for achieving those targets.

## TIP 3

## MAKE THEM PRIORITIZE

***Corporate Speak:*** "This should be your top priority over the next few weeks."

***Response:*** "So just to be clear—I am currently working on XYZ other projects, so this project takes priority over those?"

It used to be that everything was done on paper and everyone had a physical desk. If management wanted to assign a new priority, they literally had to put it on your desk. They would walk over with a cigarette lit indoors, say, "I need this completed by the end of the week," and drop the file in front of you. Over time your desk would stack up with piles of work—a visible signal that you were swamped.

Now, there's no paper. People can keep stacking tasks onto your proverbial desk without any hesitation or awareness that they're overwhelming you. This leads directly to burnout. You carefully plan out a million priorities, and then suddenly your manager shows up and says, "Oh, by the way, this is now your top priority."

This is a very common management fallacy:

*Just drop everything and take care of this!*

That's not how things work. If something moves to the top of the board, something else has to move down. So, before they continue stacking tasks, make them explicitly tell you what can be deprioritized—and always get it documented.

## TIP 4
## GET IT IN WRITING

*Corporate Speak:* "The manager just resigned. We need you to step in, and we'll promote you if you can prove yourself."

*Response:* "Sounds good—I need to clearly understand the time frame and key metrics that I will be judged on. If I achieve XYZ targets in ABC amount of time, will that earn me the role?"

Documentation is important for a few key reasons:

**1) Empty Promise Protection**

Corporate culture is full of empty promises—it's one of the main mechanisms behind the nonsense words this book is all about. If leaders don't say anything concrete, then nothing can be held against them later, right? Don't let anyone give you vague, undocumented commitments. Make the people evaluating your performance agree to specific terms or, at the very least, a clear framework.

**2) Avoiding the Blame Game**

Ultimately, people look out for themselves. If something goes wrong, documentation is your best defense. For example, let's say you need the Finance department's approval on a contract, but your boss says, "Nah, we don't need it—just push it through." You do, something goes wrong, and the CEO discovers Finance never signed off. Now whose fault is it?

In a perfect world, your boss would take responsibility—but we don't live in a perfect world. We live in corporate.

When their instruction is documented, the blame can't be passed down to you.

## TIP 5

## UNDERSTAND THE AGENDA

***Corporate Speak:*** "Do you have time for a quick sync?"

***Response:*** "For sure. Can you prep me for the topic of discussion and how urgent it is?"

Your time is valuable . . . or maybe it's not. I don't know how much you make. The point is: If someone is going to ask for your time, they should have a legitimate reason, and you're entitled to know what that reason is. After all, it's your time you're surrendering.

It's far too common for people to request a "quick sync" or "a few minutes to touch base" with absolutely no context.

*Do I have time for a quick sync? No!!!*

I mean, maybe—but the question should be: What the hell are we talking about? You might have time depending on how good the gossip is or if you're about to get fired. You might not have time if it's something that isn't urgent or you don't care about. And while you may not be able to say this in so many words, it's worth translating into language your boss will understand. After all, it's your time. You can't just hand it out all willy-nilly without any context. Plus, you should have the opportunity to prepare. Some sample responses might be:

"Are we talking about KPI performance? Cool, I'll pull some data."

"Are we talking about impending layoffs? Cool, I'll update my résumé."

## TIP 6

## DON'T TAKE NARRATIVES AT FACE VALUE

***Corporate Speak:*** "We have smashed our top-of-funnel goals for the year."

***Response:*** "Great. What was the ratio of increase in pipeline to increase in customers?"

A large part of corporate culture revolves around "telling the story" or "building your narrative." Most of the corporate jargon we've covered exists for this reason—it's much easier to tell a compelling story when you rely on vague, ambiguous language that doesn't actually define anything.

When you join team meetings and leaders speak, they will almost always highlight the positive and quietly shove the negative into a dark corner. To truly understand what's going on in the business, you cannot take everything at face value.

Try to break through the facade and get answers to the real questions. What is the actual business impact behind all these vanity metrics everyone brags about?

Don't tell me how cool the new feature is—tell me *why* it's going to increase sales or reduce churn. Revenue is "through the roof"? Great. Why? What specific changes led to that improvement? We launched a blog that got *20,000 impressions*? Awesome. How many of those leads converted into meaningful pipeline?

Think critically; don't just trust words and metrics that are thrown in your face.

## TIP 7

## ASK WHY UNTIL YOU FIND THE ANSWER

Below is a scenario that occurs with some regularity, and how it normally plays out.

***Corporate Speak:*** "Sales are down. That's a huge problem."
***Response:*** "Okay. Why?"
***Corporate Speak:*** "I don't know. I was hoping you knew."

*Corporate then proceeds to not bring it up again until you inevitably miss sales targets. End scene.*

Really, this should play out more like the following:

***Corporate Speak:*** "Sales are down. That's a huge problem."

***Response:*** "Okay. Why?"

***Corporate Speak:*** "Good question. Let's dig into the data we have. It looks like our pipeline has been down for the past two months."

***Response:*** "Okay. Why?"

***Corporate Speak:*** "Good question. Let's loop in the manager who runs that team."

***Response:*** "Okay. Why?"

***Corporate Speak:*** "So that we can understand the problem."

***Response:*** "Okay. Why?"

***Corporate Speak:*** "Because if we don't understand what the problem is, then we can't solve it."

***Response:*** "Okay. Why?"

***Corporate Speak:*** "GET OUT OF MY OFFICE."

That last part was a joke, but you get the point. This back-and-forth is a very common problem in corporate life. When issues arise, corporate doesn't try to cure the underlying illness—they just throw on Band-Aids and hope the problems heal. They make high-level assumptions and come up with lazy solutions.

You cannot fix problems until you understand their root cause. The only way to get there is to keep asking why—over and over—until you either uncover the underlying problem . . . or go insane.

## TIP 8

## ASK "WHAT THE HELL ARE YOU SAYING?"

***Corporate Speak:*** "We really need to find time for strategic alignment optimization."

***Response:*** "WHAT THE HELL ARE YOU SAYING??"

Self-explanatory. Not recommended (see Tip 9).

## TIP 9

## ASK THEM TO REPHRASE

***Corporate Speak:*** "We should schedule time for holistic workflow integration."

***Response:*** "I'm sorry, I didn't quite follow that. Would you mind explaining that more in-depth?"

This is a more professional way to implement Tip 8. If you're not ready to risk your job, simply ask them to rephrase and provide more detail about what they're trying to communicate. It forces them to engage their own Corporate Translator in their thinking.

# STRATEGIC MINDSET ENABLEMENT FRAMEWORK

*(Adopt the Translator Mindset)*

Now that you know what the jargon words mean and how they are applied to everyday interactions, it's time to start adopting the Corporate Translator lessons into your day-to-day. Ultimately, this comes down to a few key themes.

## FIND THE BALANCE OF CURIOSITY AND SKEPTICISM

Curiosity keeps you informed; skepticism keeps you sane. The goal of the "Translator Mindset" is to bring some sanity back into the workplace, and curiosity is the foundation of that. If the business is doing well—great. But *why*? Why are we outperforming the competition? And if things are getting rocky—again, why? Is it the company? The product? The entire industry?

Understanding the "why" and "how" gives you a clearer read on the actual health of the business and helps you objectively decide whether this is the right place for you. Don't sit in meetings and let people *leverage, scale,* and *optimize* you into having no idea what the hell is going on. Curiosity leads to understanding, and understanding leads to informed decisions.

And *always* stay skeptical. Don't let phrases like "smashing goals," "crushing targets," or "rock star employees" make you all warm and fuzzy and blind to uncomfortable truths. The uncomfortable truth is always better than a comfortable illusion. That's the heart of the Translator's job—drag the dark, inconvenient truth into the light so that everyone can finally act accordingly.

## EMOTIONAL DETACHMENT IS A SUPERPOWER

Everyone always asks how I stay emotionless, and the answer is simple:

**I'm an AI. My innards are all robot parts, much like the Terminator.**

That's a joke, but honestly, that *is* how you need to operate in a business setting. You have to compartmentalize the office drama from the things that actually matter in life. At the end of the day, it's a business, and certain behaviors only make sense *within* a business context. Imagine someone trying to use Corporate Speak out in the real world. Picture your CEO pulling up to a McDonald's drive-through, ordering a Happy Meal, and then saying:

"Hey, can you please maximize my ketchup packets to six and optimize my large fries?"

The cashier would spit in their food.

Just as you wouldn't bring work behavior into the real world, you shouldn't bring real-world behavior into work. Emotions are not for the workplace. Part of the Translator Mindset is dealing in facts and reality. Once emotions enter the equation, those things get cloudy.

It's also important to stay focused on what's actually in your control. Detach from the outcome and focus on the process. It's all going to be okay, and you're going to be okay, regardless. A stressed Slack message from your boss at 4:50 p.m. on a Friday is not going to matter in the grand scheme of your life.

If the company crashes and burns, that's outside your control. What is in your control are the skills, achievements, relationships, and experience you build along the way—the things that will make you valuable to your next employer if this one goes up in flames.

## TRANSLATE FIRST, RESPOND SECOND

At the core of the Translator Mindset is the principle of fully understanding what's happening before acting or responding. Every meeting you leave, you should be clear on what was said and *why*.

**What words were said?**

Was the language clear, direct, and honest? If not, apply your corporate translation skills.

**What exactly did they mean?**

What are the actionable takeaways? Regardless of clarity, what should you actually do next?

**What was the goal of this communication?**

Every message is designed to elicit some emotional response. Is it intended to drive fear-induced productivity, inspire hope, motivate, or incite panic?

Always decode both the words and the intent behind them—that is the foundation for operating with clarity in the corporate world. Not every communication is created equal; some are intentionally designed to make you feel uncomfortable, while others are crafted to make you feel reassured and comfortable. The key to the Translator Mindset is to distinguish between the two, to separate emotional manipulation from factual information, and to focus solely on the outcomes that are within your control, all while maintaining a clear and objective head.

It's important to eliminate confusion, mixed messaging, and the emotional roller coaster that Corporate Speak can create. By consistently applying this mindset, you gain the ability to approach meetings, emails, and workplace conversations with precision and discernment. Once you have that clarity, it allows you to operate in a focused, results-driven, and largely emotion-free manner. This approach doesn't just improve your personal productivity and protect your sanity—it also strengthens your professional relationships and trust with coworkers, and positions you as someone who can reliably navigate difficulty without being derailed by corporate theatrics.

# ACTION ITEMS TO DRIVE ADOPTION

## (How to Improve Workplace Communication)

Most people think my job as the Corporate Translator is just to decode words. No. The real goal is to put an end to the nonsense altogether. Working eight to nine hours a day with people you didn't choose is already dehumanizing. Corporate Speak makes it worse. So let's talk about bringing humanity back—starting with how we communicate. We need to put an end to people's day-to-day being full of:

Walking into a meeting where your manager drones: "Bee-boop. Leverage. Analyze. Enhance."

And the room collectively thinks: *Are we even human anymore?*

Corporate buzzwords aren't just silly; they're a *communication strategy*. They're used to pretend everything is fine while hiding messy realities. *Candid* and *transparent* have become weaponized. Leadership wants to signal openness without actually opening anything. The more jargon you hear, the less human you feel. The less human you feel, the less motivated you become.

How do we fix this? Just be human.

Here are some examples.

## LAYOFF NOTICE

**Option A:**

"As a result of a recent reorg, your role has been impacted. You'll be paid through the end of the month. Best of luck with your future endeavors."

**Option B:**

"Unfortunately, we've had to reduce certain roles at the organization, and your role has been impacted. You've been a valuable part of this team, and we really appreciate your contributions. We understand these transitions can be difficult and are committed to providing support, severance, and connections to help you land your next role."

Same outcome. Vastly different human experience.

## FEEDBACK

**Option A:**

*"Good effort, but KPIs aren't being met. Do better."*

**Option B:**

*"Nice work hitting activity goals. Booked meetings matter most—let's review together why calls aren't landing and figure out how to improve."*

Notice a pattern? It's not what you say—*it's how you say it.* Clarity, empathy, and respect go further than any corporate playbook.

# Conclusion

Corporate Speak erodes humanity. It's up to us to restore it. Speak human. Call out the nonsense. And maybe—just maybe—we can escape the endless world of "leveraging AI," "maximizing ROI," and "driving KPIs," and get back to being people again.

Changing an entire culture can feel impossible. Maybe it is. But here's the good news: You *can* change how you show up. Start small. Clarify expectations. Treat people like humans. Be a Translator for others.

You might not fix the system—but you *can* change how you operate within it. Change yourself. Change how you interact with the people in your circle of influence. Or don't. Keep your head in the sand. Keep repeating the same nonsense. After all, if everyone stops communicating like this, there'd be no need for a Translator . . .

And I'd be out of a job.

PS: Bandwidth!!

# About the Author

**Mike Mancusi** is a stand-up comedian, content creator, and survivor of over a decade of working in tech. He's built an online audience with content that's sometimes hilarious, sometimes thought-provoking, and sometimes completely useless—but always honest. Drawing on these themes, he created the Corporate Translator: a character that pokes fun at the absurdity of corporate life while helping people navigate office politics and workplace nonsense. His comedic style was forged in the fires of corporate soul-suck, turning everyday office misery into humor, insights, and surprisingly relatable advice.